Sainsbury Centre for Visual Arts

The Deutsche Bibliothek holds
a record for this publication in the
Deutsche Nationalbibliografie;
detailed bibliographical data can
be found under http://dnb.ddb.de

Library of Congress Control
Number is available

Prestel Verlag, A Member
of Verlagsgruppe Random
House GmbH

Prestel Verlag
Königinstrasse 9
80539 Munich
Germany
Tel +49 (089) 242908-300
Fax +49 (089) 242908-355
www.prestel.de

Prestel Publishing
900 Broadway, Suite 603
New York NY 10003
USA
Tel +1 (212) 995-2720
Fax +1 (212) 995-2733

Prestel Publishing Ltd
4 Bloomsbury Place
London
WC1A 2QA
UK
Tel +44 (020) 7323-5004
Fax +44 (020) 7636-8004
www.prestel.com

ISBN 978-3-7913-4492-8

Sainsbury Centre for Visual Arts Foster + Partners

Norman Foster
Kenneth Powell

PRESTEL
MUNICH ▪ BERLIN ▪ LONDON ▪ NEW YORK

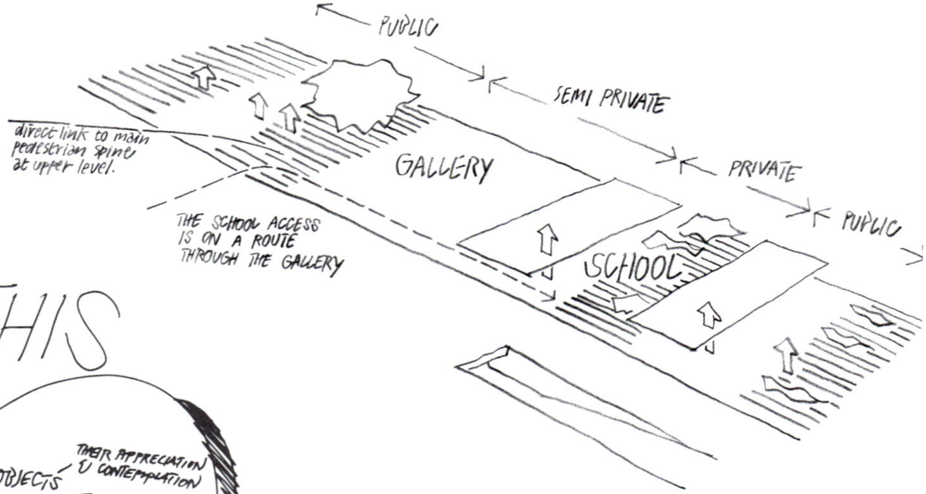
PUBLIC
SEMI PRIVATE
PRIVATE
PUBLIC
direct link to main
pedestrian spine
at upper level.
GALLERY
THE SCHOOL ACCESS
IS ON A ROUTE
THROUGH THE GALLERY
SCHOOL

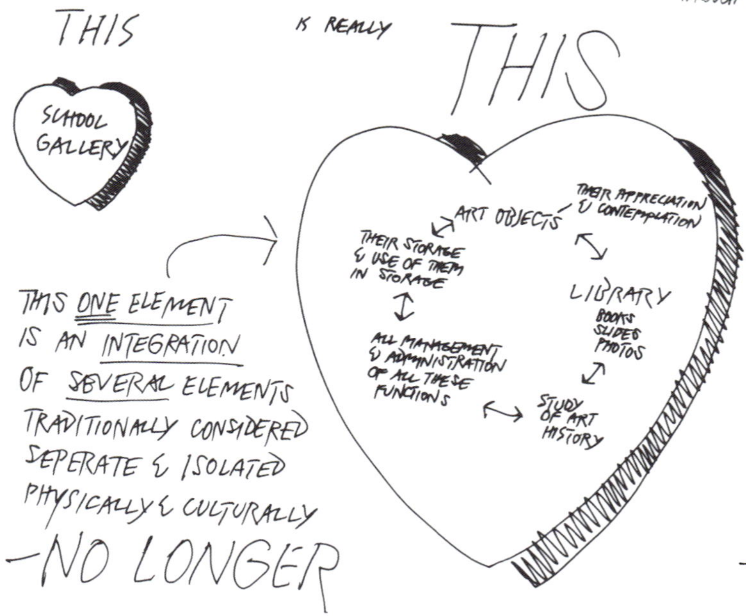
THIS
SCHOOL
GALLERY
IS REALLY
THIS
ART OBJECTS
THEIR APPRECIATION
& CONTEMPLATION
THEIR STORAGE
& USE OF THEM
IN STORAGE
LIBRARY
BOOKS
SLIDES
PHOTOS
ALL MANAGEMENT
& ADMINISTRATION
OF ALL THESE
FUNCTIONS
STUDY
OF ART
HISTORY
THIS ONE ELEMENT
IS AN INTEGRATION
OF SEVERAL ELEMENTS
TRADITIONALLY CONSIDERED
SEPERATE & ISOLATED
PHYSICALLY & CULTURALLY
—NO LONGER

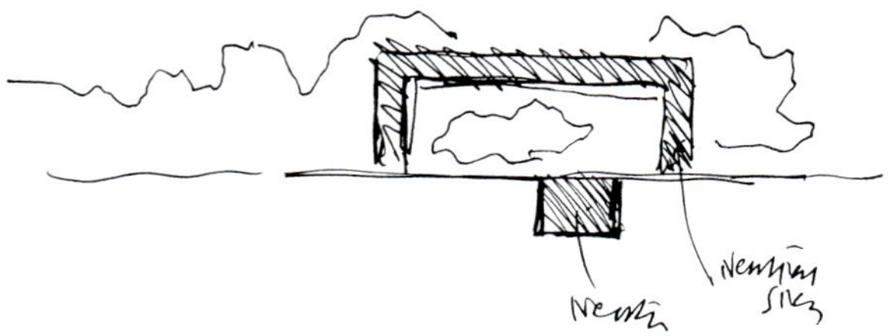

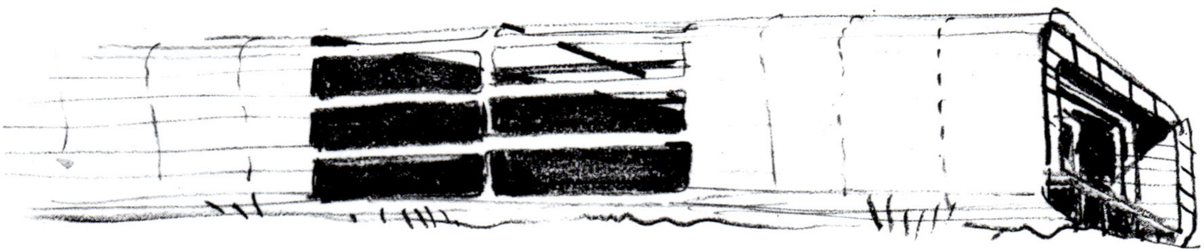

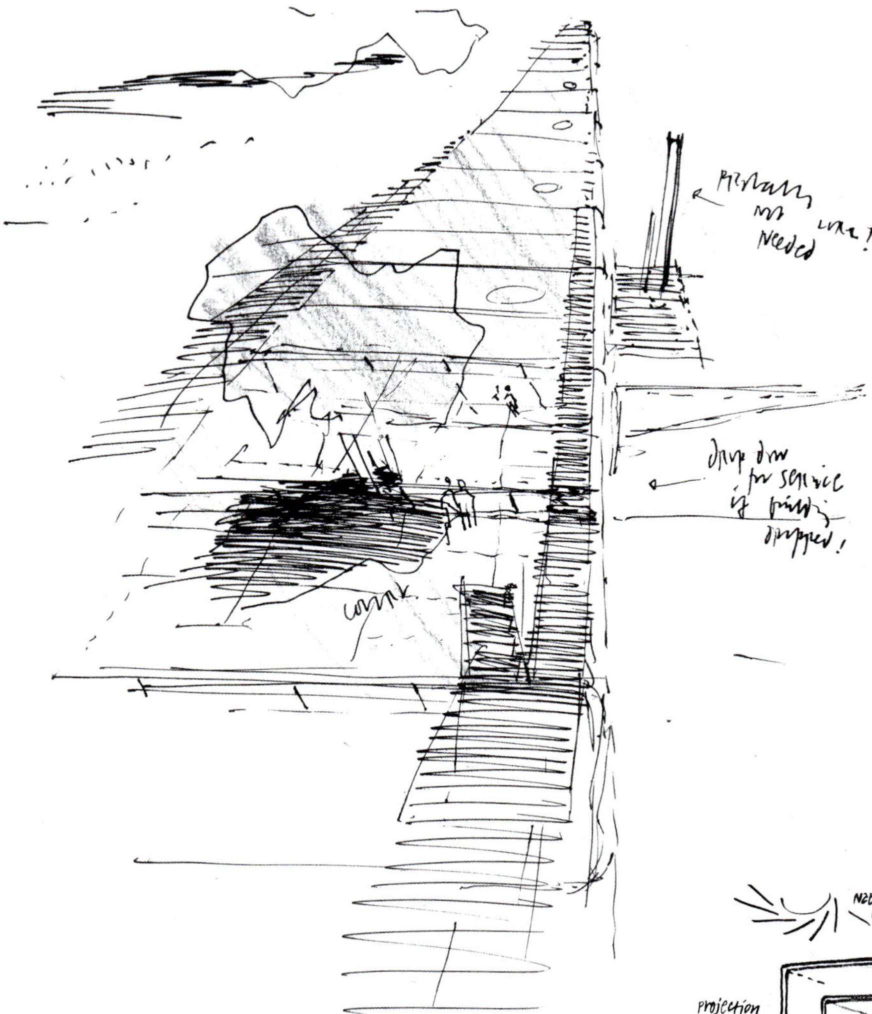

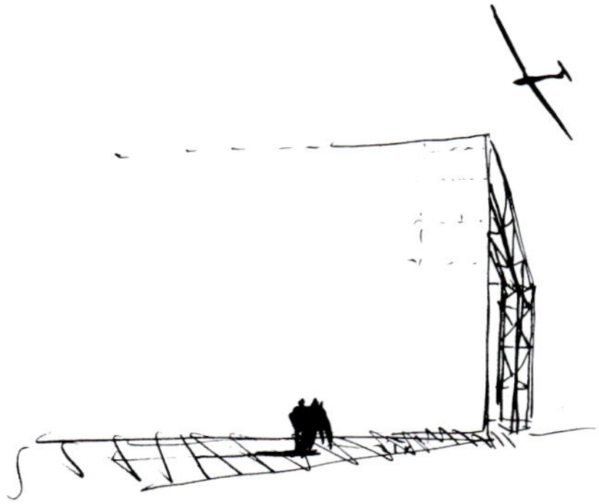

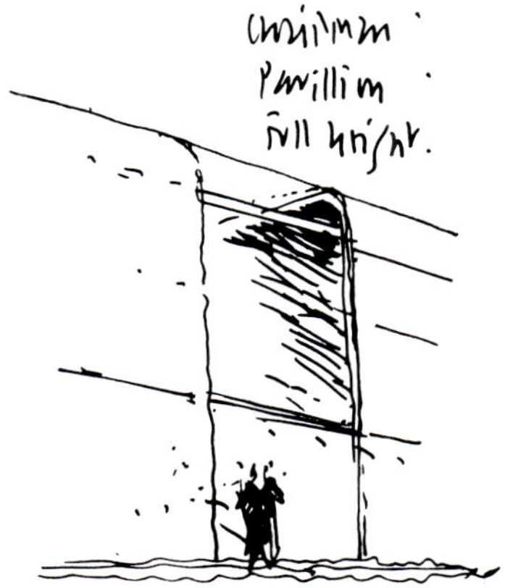

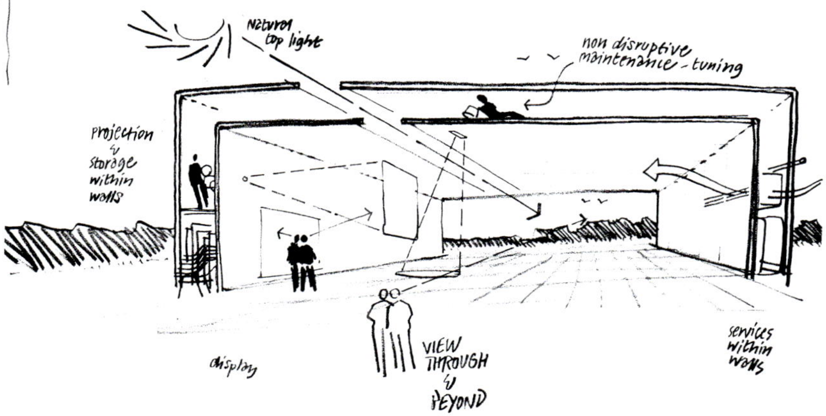

In these early sketches Norman Foster begins to outline a vision of the Sainsbury Centre as an integrated, flexible container – a gallery without walls in the conventional sense.

Overleaf: The gallery 'living area', seen shortly after completion in 1978.

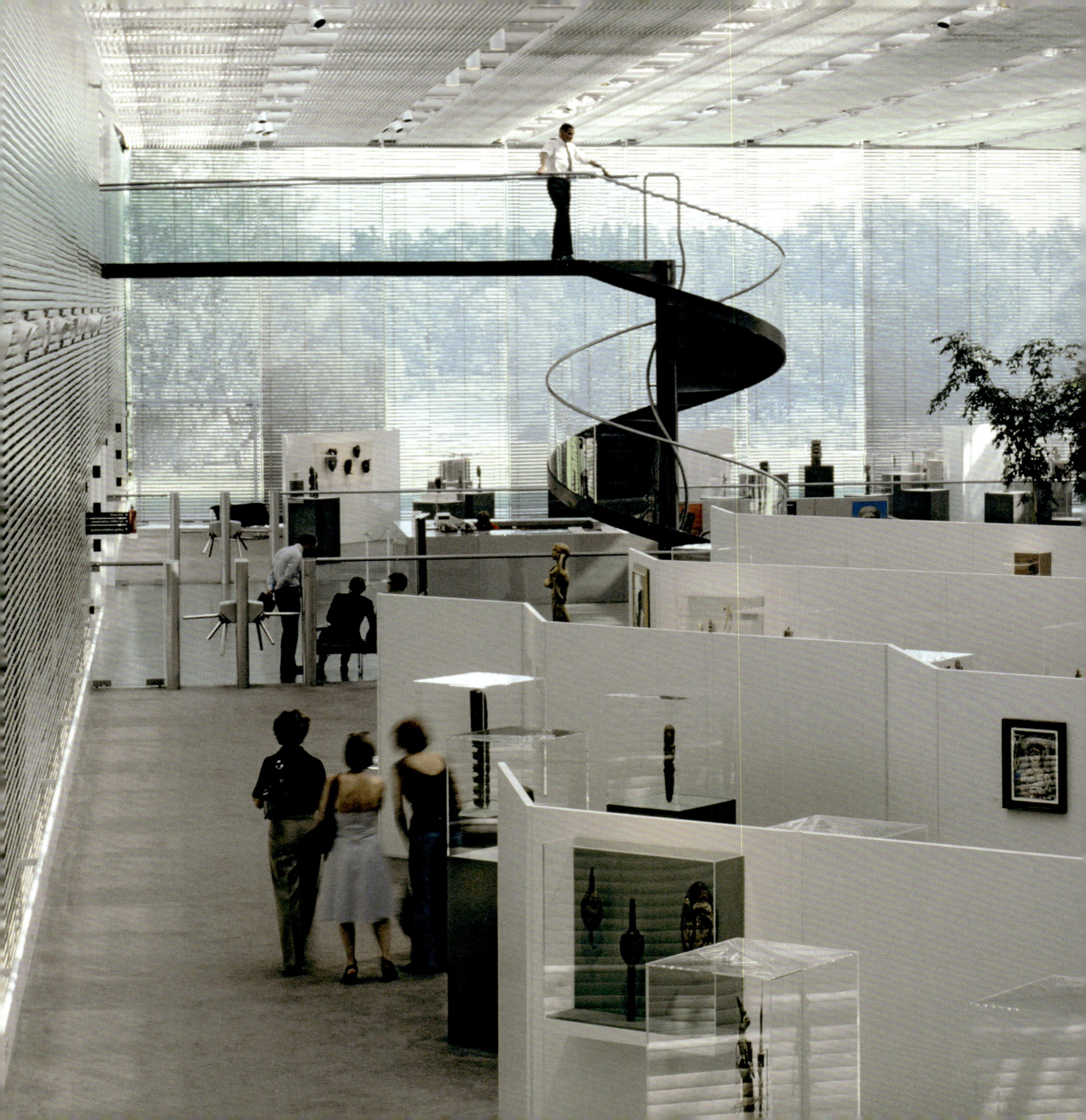

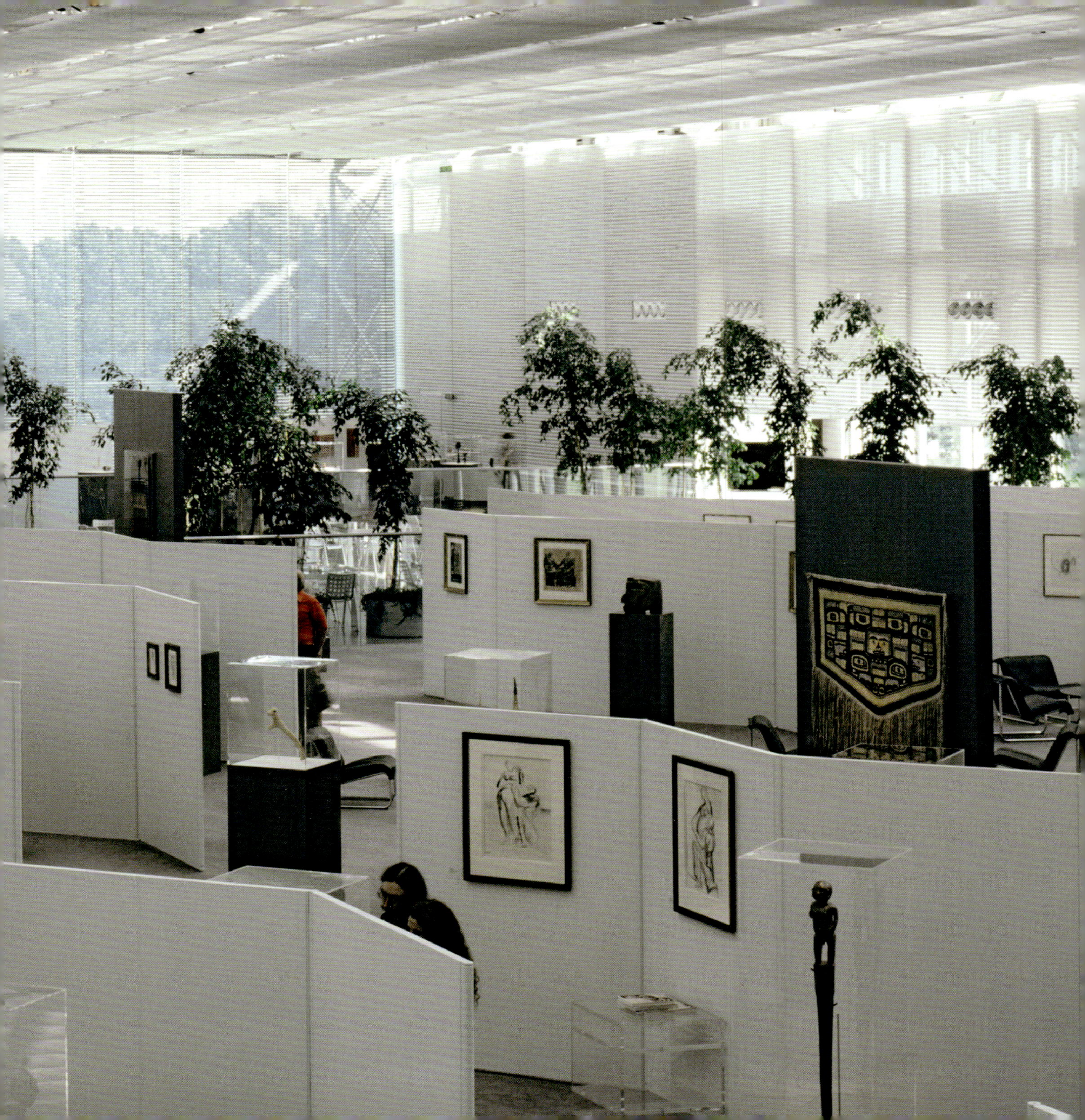

Introduction Norman Foster

The story of this project begins in November 1973, with Sir Robert and Lady Sainsbury's decision to give their extraordinary collection of ethnographic and twentieth-century art to the University of East Anglia, together with an endowment for a new building. Although they were not to know it at the time, this initiative would lead to the Centre for Visual Arts. Much more than a gallery, it was to be a new academic and social focus within the university campus.

For me, the starting point was an invitation for 'a brief discussion' with Sir Robert Sainsbury on New Year's Day 1974, at the Sainsburys' house in Smith Square. As it turned out, that discussion carried on through lunch, when I met Lisa Sainsbury, and continued until the end of the day.

I left that meeting with three strong impressions. First their home, which was modest, intimate and discreet; every space was married with extraordinary works of art. Sir Robert's study had been designed by a young Dutch-Indonesian architect, Kho Liang Ie. Here there were works by anonymous artists – tiny Eskimo carvings, for example – objects that at the time of their acquisition were barely recognised as works of art in the traditional sense.

The second impression was the contrast between this elegant couple and the radical nature of some of the art. Hanging over the fireplace was a portrait of Lady Sainsbury by Francis Bacon, which was almost shocking. Bacon, like Moore and Giacometti was virtually unknown at the time that the Sainsburys became patrons. The third impression was how those first conversations ranged so far and wide – I gained clues about their way of looking at things and I do not mean visually: it was as radical as those progressive artists they had encouraged.

It was clear that we had a shared distaste for the monumental and a belief that studying works of art should be a pleasurable aesthetic experience. There was a philosophy, which underpinned the gift, that the building should encourage as many people as possible to view the collection. If such a building could also be a meeting place and provide a link to academic areas, then so much the better. Beyond these headlines the brief did not really exist. The first design exercise was to develop a schedule for a project which, so far as we were aware, had no social precedent.

One of the first decisions was where to site the building within Sir Denys Lasdun's campus – there were many preconceptions from various quarters about where it should be. On my first visit to the university I was shown a site next to the music school, with the intention of grouping the arts together. Ultimately, after many studies, I chose a more remote site next to the scientists. That seemed absolutely in the spirit of the gift: the avoidance of an arts ghetto – the equivalent in university terms of a South Bank. I consulted Sir Denys and aligned the axis on the campus' 45-degree geometry. The building's orientation and glazing are such that views out frame the lake in one direction and woodland in the other, to create the impression of idyllic isolation.

An early strategic decision concerned the form of the building itself. The brief could have produced a number of separate pavilions – that would have been the obvious response. A strong link between the collection and the temporary exhibition space could have produced one unit; another would have been a school for the history of art. Add to that a restaurant and senior common room, and there was the potential for at least three buildings. I finally made the leap to say that the linkage between all those elements was so strong that the case for integrating them within a single enclosure was overwhelming.

The resultant space is a gallery without walls in the conventional sense. Although it reads as a single volume, there are in reality four main areas for display and related circulation. Arrival via the bridge and internal stair or through the main entrance is into a conservatory, which originally combined the functions of reception, security and café, and later incorporated a bookshop. To one side of the conservatory was a space for special exhibitions, to the other the 'living area': a name that expresses the spirit of the place with its easy chairs, low tables and books on art for relaxed contemplation of the collection – a conscious echo of its original domestic setting.

The nature of the gallery, with its complementary range of uses – public and private, academic and recreational, formal and relaxed – gave it a very special atmosphere. One critic has characterised it as an 'urban room' – like a city space in microcosm – something quite unheard of within an arts building.

If 'integration' was a guiding principle, so too was 'flexibility'. I wanted to ensure that individual areas could be reconfigured as needs changed, or the environment be adjusted to suit the demands of a particular exhibition. There was also the recognition that items such as the mechanical services, would have a relatively short life – very much like an aircraft, where the airframe may be capable of flying many thousands of hours while the engines and avionics will be replaced several times during its lifetime.

The system of tubular supporting structure and related panels, enclosing the roof and walls, was also developed with flexibility in mind. There are three types of panels – glazed, solid and perforated – which are interchangeable by undoing six bolts. Any panel can be changed quickly from solid to glass or vice versa. We were able to use this in-built flexibility to advantage ten years later, when the cladding was replaced with an upgraded product. Kenneth Powell examines the history of this change in his following essay.

Looking up from inside the 'living area' one sees a structure that gently filters daylight. This walk-in zone enables the gallery lighting to be changed or focused easily. All the ductwork and plant that might otherwise occupy the roof space has been located discreetly within the double-skin or in an undercroft. The double walls absorb toilet blocks, draught lobbies and other ancillary spaces that would otherwise compromise the clarity of the gallery. The concept of the undercroft was developed further at Stansted Airport, where we effectively turned the conventional airport terminal upside down. There, the undercroft houses all the machinery that drives the building while the roof canopy draws in daylight. The Stansted model has since been adopted for a new generation of airports worldwide, including our own terminals in Hong Kong and Beijing, so in that sense, as in other ways, the Sainsbury Centre was an influential turning point.

The building was also ahead of its time as a pioneer of low-energy design. We strove to create a series of spaces in which the lighting and temperature could be adjusted without using complex mechanical systems. In fact, the building was a considered attempt to design out mechanical refrigeration. Apart from a later lecture space, there was no cooling as such. We worked from the principle that the collection, built up over forty years, had previously been displayed in a country house or a London town house, so why should it now need to go into a refrigerator?

I also have a particular passion for natural light and am fascinated by the way in which it constantly changes, and how that can inform and enhance the spaces and the way one experiences them. Again our reference point was the domestic setting. Apart from a few sensitive items, most of the collection can be viewed in subdued daylight, just as it had been in the Sainsburys' home; even a glimpse of controlled sunlight is encouraged at certain times of the day.

The louvres that line the interior are electronically controlled, so when the sun comes out they open or close depending on the settings. The technology is relatively simple, but it is still a very sensitive machine with very positive levels of control. In the temporary exhibitions gallery, which looks out towards the lake through the glazed end wall, the blinds can be lowered completely to reduce light levels as required.

The quality of the architecture owes much to the driving force of the patrons behind it. I have described Sir Robert and Lady Sainsbury as our toughest clients – and that is the ultimate compliment. They made incredible efforts to join us in the research, to question and to support. It is not surprising then that the building should challenge preconceptions about museums.

It is perhaps also not surprising that Sir Robert and Lady Sainsbury – and more recently Lord Sainsbury – should maintain a strong involvement with the Centre. It thrived from its opening in 1978. Over time, however, the benefits of additional facilities were identified, not least the way in which they would enable the Centre to broaden its activities. In 1988, a new gift from the Sainsbury family allowed the building to be extended, creating display space for the reserve collection, together with additional curatorial and conservation facilities and a flexible space for exhibitions and conferences.

In adding to a modular building that is literally 'open-ended', an obvious move would have been to extend it in one or both directions. However, the Sainsburys argued for an alternative approach because they both loved the building as it was. I was totally in sympathy with that view, which was an incentive to find a radical alternative. The new wing therefore extends the building at undercroft level, exploiting the contours of the site to emerge in the form of a glazed 'Crescent' incised into the landscape. From outside there is just a hint at what lies beneath: only from the lake is the full extent of the new wing apparent in a silvery sweep of glass.

In 2004 a further gift allowed a programme of improvements to be undertaken. We created additional display spaces and an education centre, and formed an internal link between the original building and the Crescent Wing. We also took the opportunity to recast the bookshop, café and other visitor facilities.

Alongside our own interventions, it is interesting to chart other ways in which the building has adapted over time – quite independently of any design input. It becomes a conference centre in the summer, a venue for wedding receptions at weekends, and a setting for formal dinners, which combine occasionally with new exhibitions, reflecting quite unexpected patterns of use. In that sense, the Sainsbury Centre is the opposite of a static entity, frozen in time in some imagined state of completion or perfection. Instead, it is a living and evolving project – just as Sir Robert and Lady Sainsbury imagined it would be.

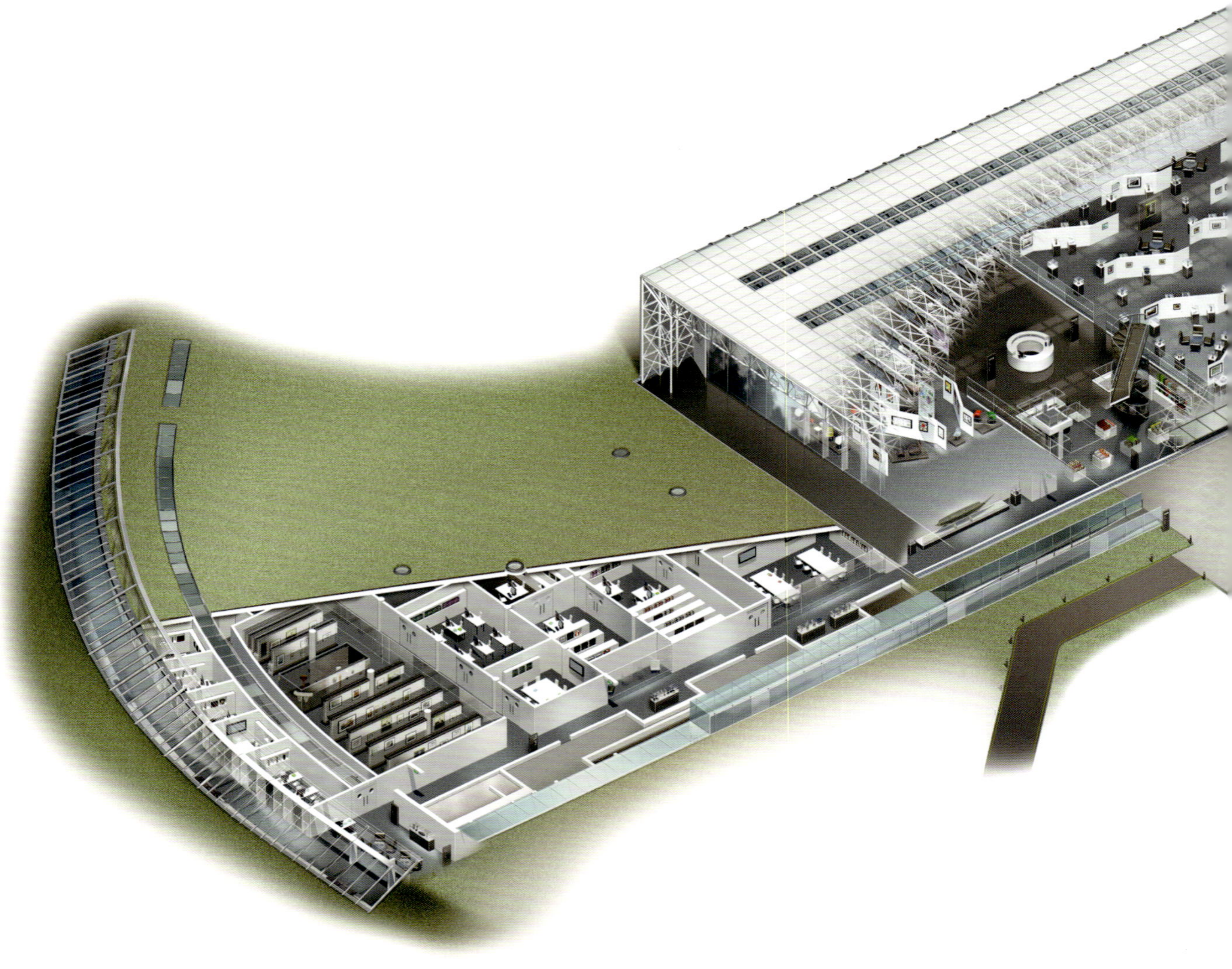

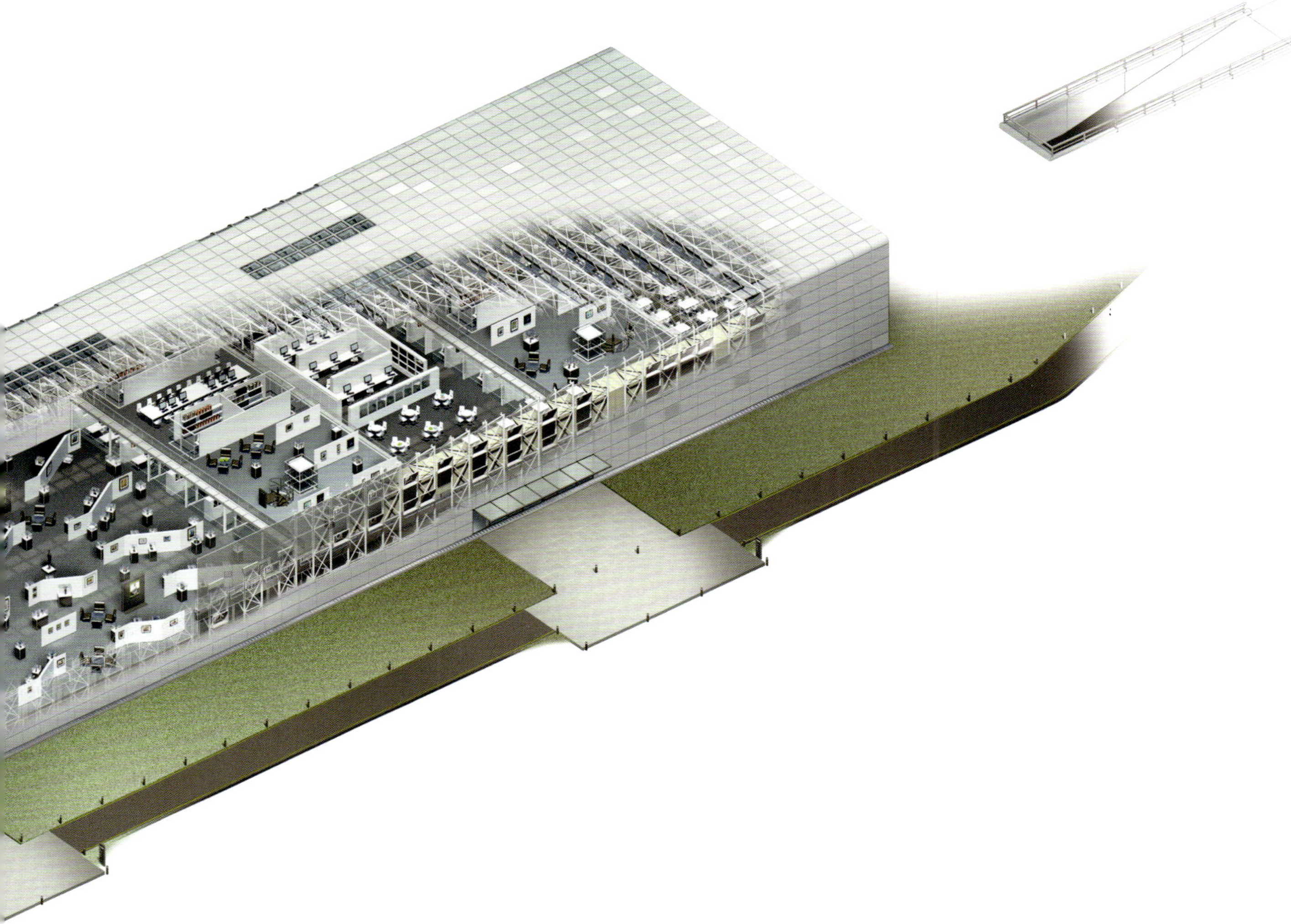

In this cutaway drawing, the relationship between the gallery areas and the various functions of the School of World Art Studies is revealed. The Crescent Wing, which added a reserve collection display, conservation laboratories and offices, is seen in the foreground.

The living museum Kenneth Powell

The Sainsbury Centre for Visual Arts, located on the campus of the University of East Anglia in Norwich, remains, more than three decades after its completion, one of Norman Foster's most satisfying and moving works. Together with the Willis Faber & Dumas building in Ipswich, completed in 1975, it established Foster as a major force on the British architectural scene – a supreme innovator who was soon to achieve global recognition with the commission to build the Hongkong and Shanghai Bank Headquarters in Hong Kong. The Bank would transform Foster's office – then known as Foster Associates – into an international practice. No longer would it be an intimate studio-based operation, with a team of no more than thirty, with Foster himself closely involved in virtually every aspect of a project. As Foster recalls, 'The Sainsbury Centre was the achievement of an exceptionally talented team; but it was also the last project on which I could see myself as the job architect, as it were, with a completely hands-on role.'

The 1970s was a troubled decade in Britain, dominated by a crippling energy crisis, and characterised by social and industrial unrest and political inertia. Architecture at that time also seemed to have lost its way. In that context, Willis Faber and the Sainsbury Centre can be seen as sensational re-statements of the capacity of modern architecture to reinvent itself in tune with the needs of a changing social and environmental order.

However, as Norman Foster always insists, there can be no great architecture without inspirational clients: 'The most successful projects share to some degree that quality of enlightened concern called patronage.' The clients for the Sainsbury Centre were two extraordinary people – Sir Robert and Lisa Sainsbury. The immediate personal chemistry between Foster and 'Bob and Lisa' as he was to know them, would lead not only to the creation of a masterwork but also to a warm and deepening friendship; indeed, Foster came to regard them 'almost as parents'.

Robert James Sainsbury (1906-2000) was the second son of John Benjamin Sainsbury whose father, John James Sainsbury, was the founder of the family grocery business. Jointly with his brother Alan, Robert had run the family business from the late 1930s until his retirement as its chairman in 1969. He had studied at Cambridge, where his principal leisure interest was bridge rather than art; in fact he claimed that he never entered an art gallery during his student years. 'Such was my upbringing and education,' he wrote 'that as a young man, I was not subjected to any art dictums and so, uninhibited, without any preconceived ideas

Right: Portraits of Sir Robert and Lady Sainsbury by Francis Bacon. The Sainsburys were among Bacon's earliest patrons.

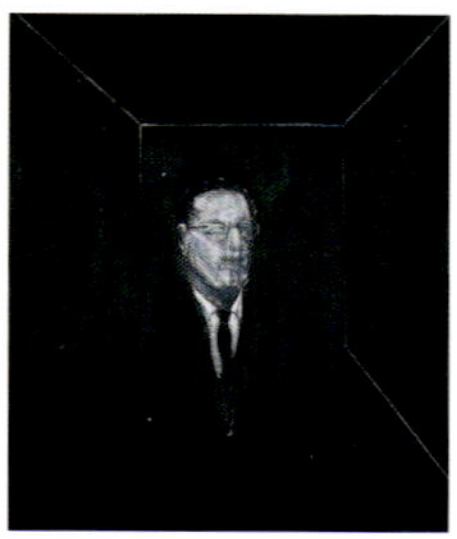

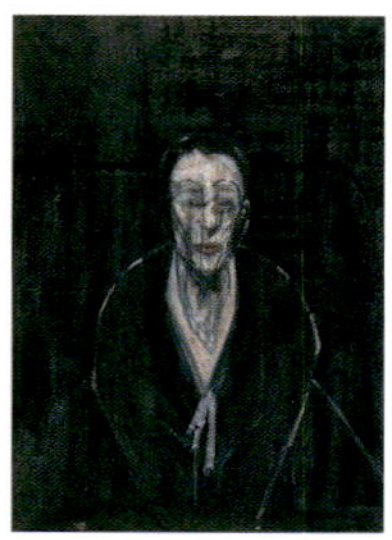

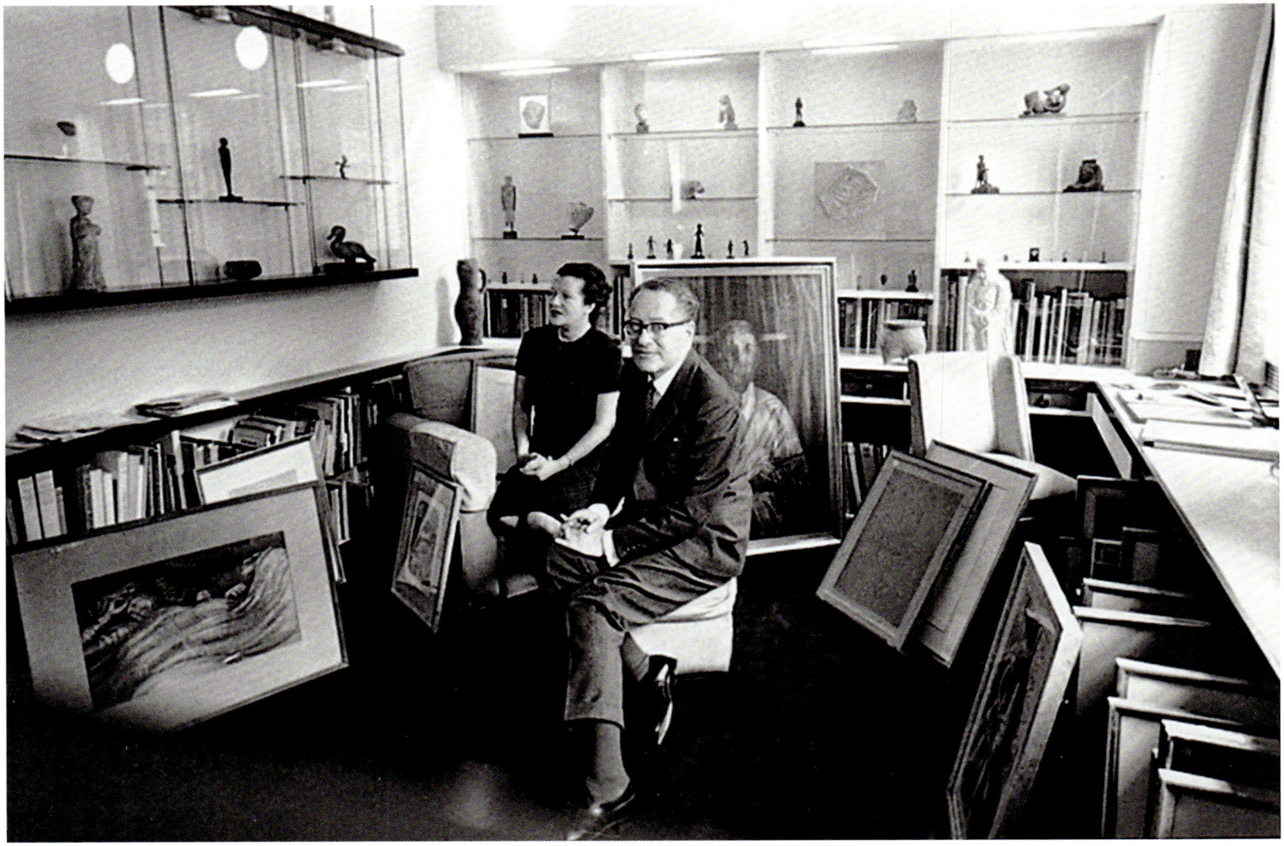

Above: Sir Robert and Lady Sainsbury photographed by Lord Snowdon in 1965 in the study of their house at 5 Smith Square. As significant figures in the London art world, Snowdon included them in his book *Private View: The Lively World of British Art.*

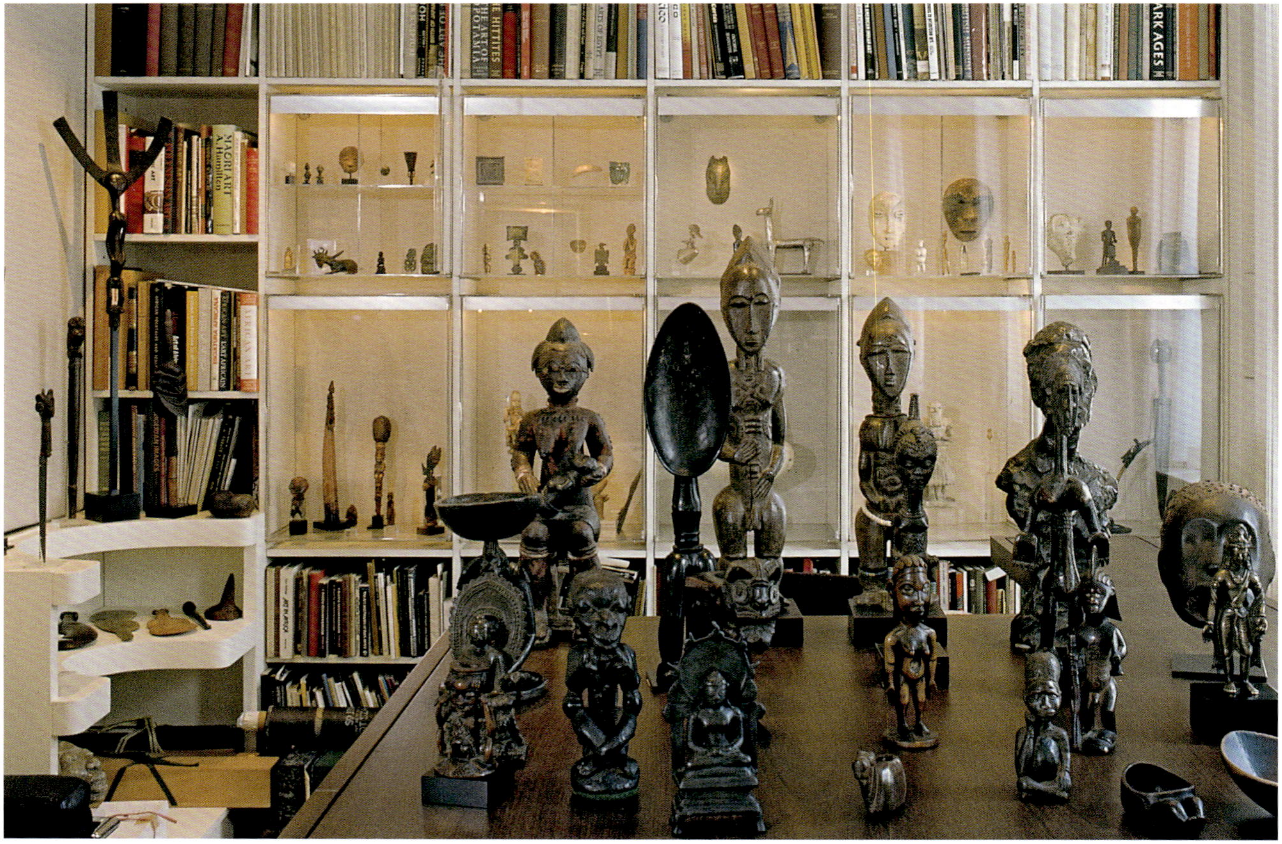

Above: A cabinet in Sir Robert Sainsbury's study, designed by Kho Liang Ie, contained smaller pieces from the collection and was known as 'the toy department'.

Right: Items from the collection at Smith Square. From left: 'Fisherman's God' figure from the Cook Islands; Henry Moore's 'Mother and Child' (1932); Egyptian mummy portrait of a youth (c. AD 100).

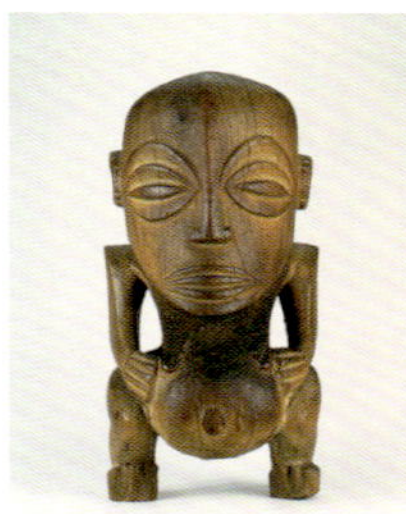

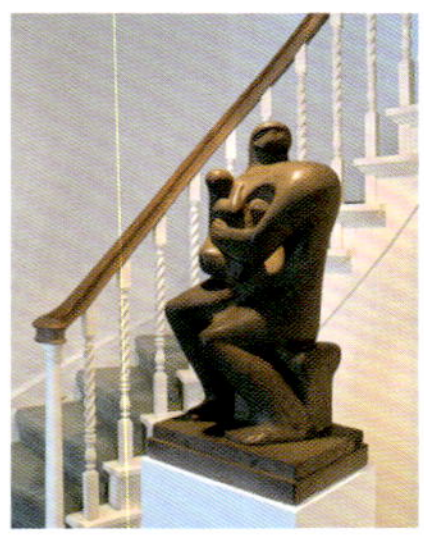

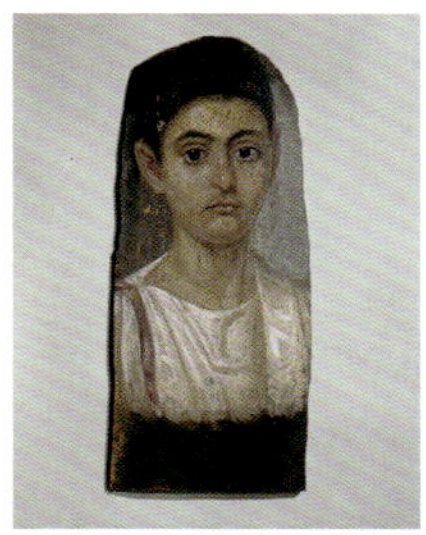

Below left: Giacometti's 'Standing Woman' (1959) in the sitting room at Smith Square. The comfortable integration of objects into this domestic setting testifies to the deeply personal nature of the collection and the pleasure that the Sainsburys derived from it.

Below right: Modigliani's 'Head of a Woman' (1918-1919), acquired by Sir Robert Sainsbury in 1935.

Right: Mexican jade mask in the Olmec style (1200-400BC).

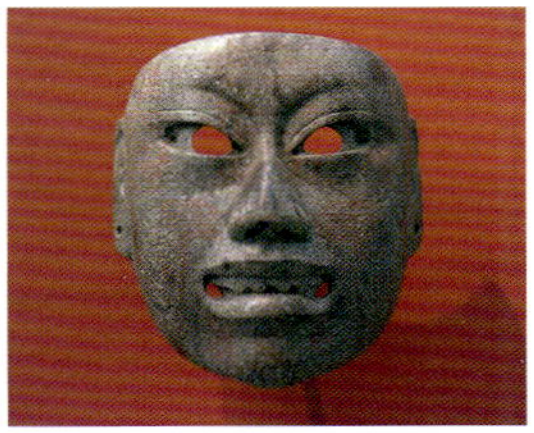

regarding the reputedly good in art, or the right way to approach a work of art, I was able to make my own discoveries.'

By the early 1930s he had developed an interest in contemporary art. Advised by friends, in particular the artist Blair Hughes-Stanton and his wife Ida Graves, Robert Sainsbury acquired sculptures by Jacob Epstein and Henry Moore. (Sainsbury helped Hughes-Stanton and Graves to establish the Gemini Press, producing exquisitely printed books.) In 1937 he married a cousin, Lisa Van den Bergh (born 1912), who was connected to the Dutch food manufacturing dynasty. Lisa Sainsbury's father was a professor at the Sorbonne and her acquaintance with the Parisian art scene doubtless widened her husband's horizons.

Sir Robert would become a collector in the sense once defined by Peggy Guggenheim as 'someone interested in art for his own self-ennoblement.' Nothing was bought merely as an investment and the sums invested were usually quite modest. Describing his approach to collecting, in his introduction to the first Sainsbury Centre catalogue, he wrote:

'I have never regarded myself as a collector in the most usually accepted sense of the word; that is to say, I have always refused to acquire something merely because it filled a gap or added to the representation of a particular art form. Rarity, as such, has had no attraction for me. If asked what I am looking for, I always say "I am not looking for anything". On the contrary, I have spent my life resisting temptation.

'For although denying that I am a collector, I have to admit that, first as a bachelor and then jointly with my wife, I have for over forty years been a "passionate acquirer": a passionate acquirer of works of art that have appealed to me, irrespective of period or style, subject only to the limitation of size – in relation to the space available – and, naturally, cash.'

Together Robert and Lisa would acquire works by Picasso, Giacometti, Modigliani and the young Francis Bacon. Indeed, Bacon was to become a major interest; in due course Bacon painted no fewer than eight portraits of Lisa, five of which, characteristically, he disliked and destroyed. A particular interest was so-called 'primitive' art from Africa, the Pacific, Asia and the Americas, which was to have a major influence on Epstein, Moore and others. Another special enthusiasm was for very small objects, including Japanese netsuke. Robert Sainsbury kept a vitrine filled with netsuke next to his bed and referred to it jokingly as the 'toy department'.

Though essentially eclectic, the Sainsbury collection falls broadly into two categories: antique

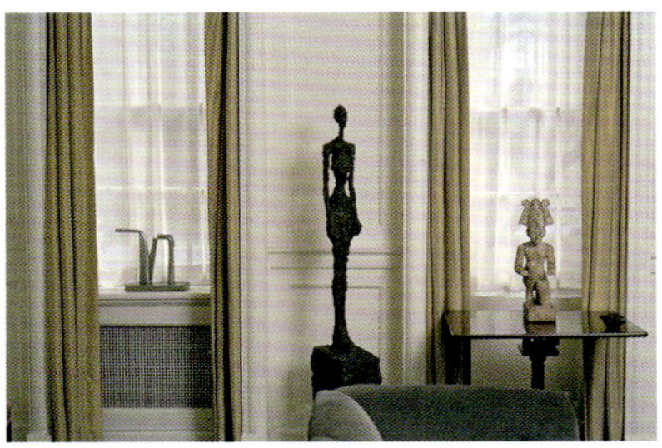

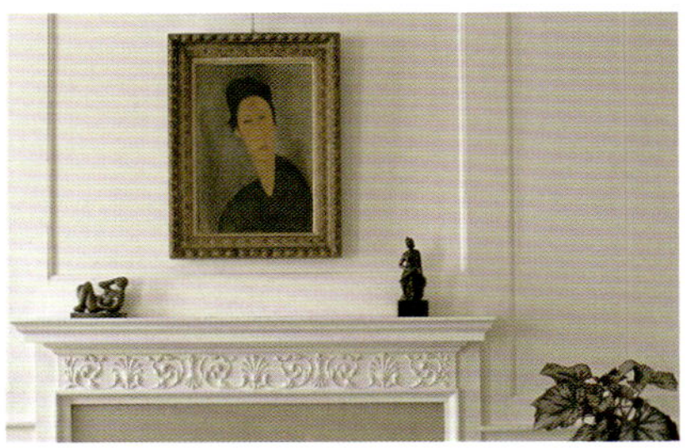

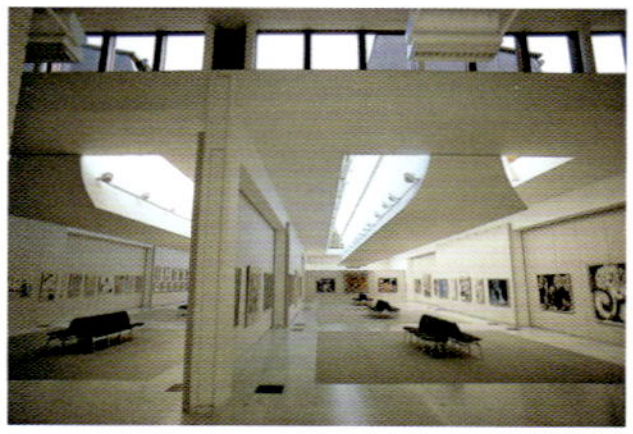

Left: Norman Foster's photograph of Alvar Aalto's ingeniously toplit Jutland Art Museum, taken on the study tour with the Sainsburys in October 1974.

or ethnic sculptural objects; and late-nineteenth and twentieth-century European art; there is an underlying anthropomorphic theme, with an emphasis on heads and figurines, which gives it an incredible coherence. Lisa Sainsbury also had a personal interest in modern studio pottery, especially the work of Lucy Rie and Hans Coper, which she began to collect in the 1950s.

By the early 1970s, with works of art filling much of their house in Smith Square, and some of it in storage at their country home in Berkshire, Robert and Lisa Sainsbury were looking at ways of preserving and displaying the collection publicly. In November 1973 they announced that they were to give some 500 works of art (a number that more than doubled over time) to the then relatively new University of East Anglia (UEA). Initially it was to be left to the university to house the collection on the still-expanding campus – a classic 1960s megastructure, designed by Sir Denys Lasdun – but the Sainsburys' son David (later Lord) Sainsbury subsequently undertook to fund a new building to contain it. Asked why the gift was to a new university and not an established institution, Sir Robert replied:

'We want to give some men and women – and who better than undergraduates in a School of Fine Art? – the opportunity to look at works of art in the natural context of their work and daily lives, not just because they have been prompted to visit a museum or art gallery. To give them the opportunity, when young, of learning the pleasures of visual experience of looking at works of art from a sensual, not only an intellectual point of view: above all, of realising that certain artefacts are works of art as well as evidence of history. A new university clearly lends itself to our project in a way not possible at the older universities.'

The Sainsburys had been considering the choice of a possible architect for some time. The Dutch-Indonesian designer Kho Liang Ie (1927-75), best known for his work at Schiphol airport, had already worked for Robert Sainsbury, designing his study and display cases at Smith Square. The Sainsburys had consulted him about the gallery project. It was proposed initially that he should be responsible for the interiors within a building designed by Foster, but Kho Liang Ie tragically died during the early stages of the scheme and Foster would in due course assume creative responsibility for the entire project.

In selecting an architect, the Sainsburys also benefited from the advice of Blair Hughes-Stanton's son Corin, a writer on design matters and editor of *Design* magazine. It was probably he who suggested a visit to Foster Associates' Fred Olsen Amenity Centre

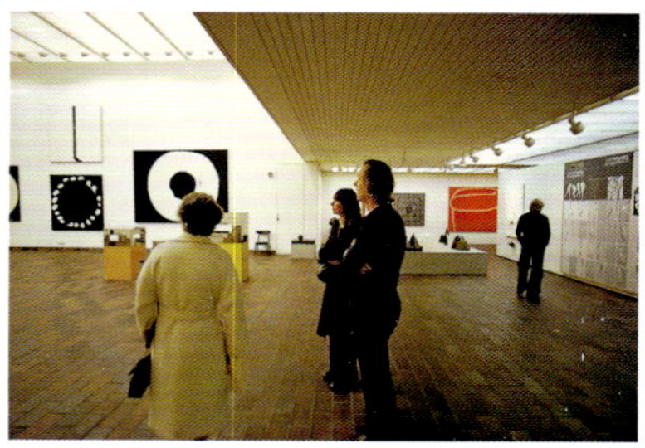

Right: Norman Foster's photograph of the Louisiana Museum of Modern Art in Denmark, taken on the study tour with the Sainsburys in October 1974. Lady Sainsbury is in the foreground, left.

at Millwall Dock, completed in 1970 and published in *Design*, which led to the meeting with Foster. Robert Sainsbury, a progressive thinker who believed that a successful business needed to care for its staff, had warmed to the architecture but also to the social agenda which the building reflected: amenities such as a canteen, showers and games room, shared by dock workers and managers alike, were a remarkable innovation at that time.

In his introduction to this book, Norman Foster recalls his first meeting with the Sainsburys, on the morning of New Year's Day 1974, and his first impressions of Smith Square: 'Every space was married with extraordinary works of art … it was a combination of exquisite taste and restraint.' What was scheduled as a brief meeting ran on to lunchtime and turned into an entire day of discussion. The Sainsburys agreed with Foster's view that a gallery should be a welcoming place, not a mausoleum. The impression of his future clients that Foster went away with was one of 'independence, openness and conviction.'

Foster's formal appointment came soon after the New Year's Day meeting and by May 1974 discussions were taking place about the brief for the building and its location on the campus. Seven possible sites were identified initially, one of them close to the Music Centre designed by Arup Associates. The seven were quickly reduced to four main strategies suitable for study, as Norman Foster describes:

'The original intention was that the building would go at the arts end of the campus, but we wanted to throw the whole thing wide open. We considered a "gateway" site for the campus and an almost subterranean building right in the middle; we looked at the arts corner and then at the site where the building finally settled. It was on a study trip – after we had visited Aalto's Museum of Modern Art at Aalborg in Jutland – that we decided that the building should be where it ended up. Everybody liked the idea that it would be next to the sciences and close to the student residences and that it would have an aspect on to the broad. There would also be no need to spend money constructing new roads and services – the masterplan indicated future growth along the line of the Yare Valley and a network of roads, drainage, water, gas and so forth had already been provided.'

Placed close to the Lasdun terraces and responding to the sawtooth geometry of the campus, yet looking away to the water and landscape beyond, the building would be able to establish its own clear identity. The location also reflected both Foster's and the Sainsburys' dislike of the idea of an 'arts ghetto'.

Right: Norman Foster's photograph of Mies van der Rohe's New National Gallery in Berlin, taken on the study tour with the Sainsburys in October 1974. Lady Sainsbury is seen right.

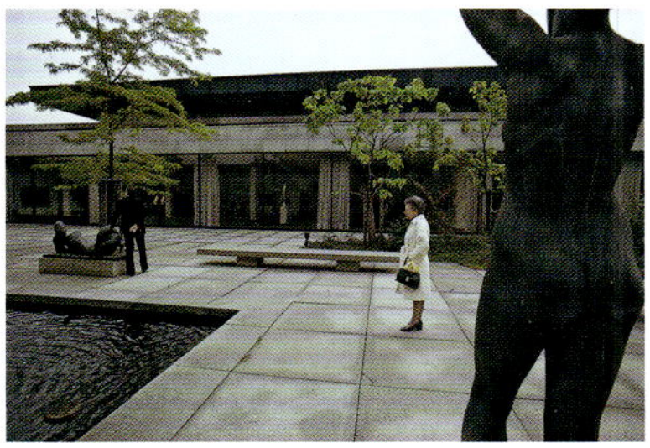

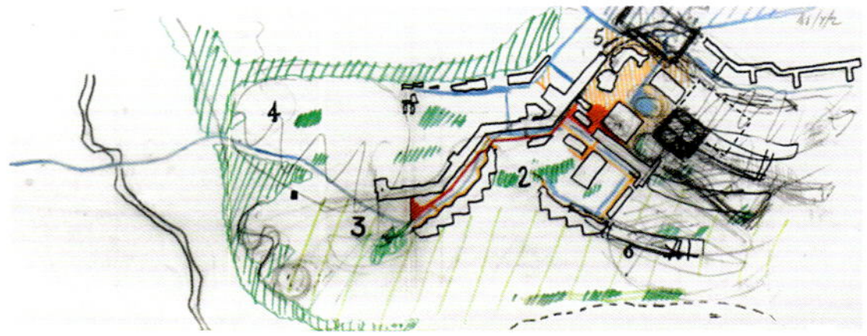

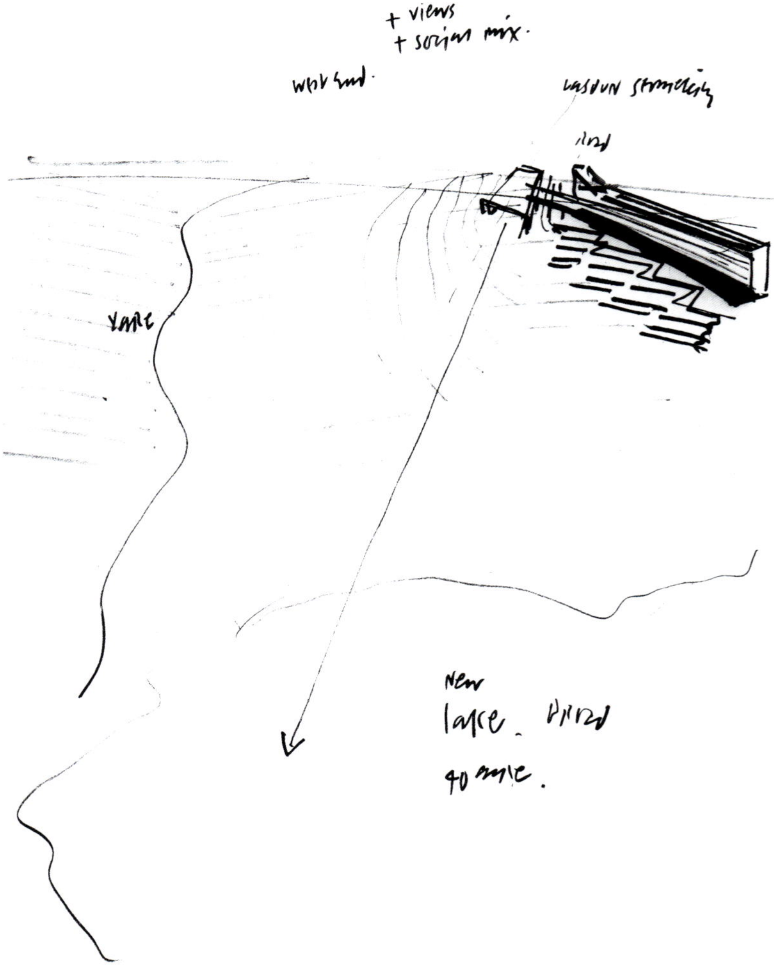

Perhaps there were also memories of the writer CP Snow's influential plea, first set out in a lecture in 1959, for the 'two cultures', of science and the arts, to be brought more closely together.

UEA's charismatic Vice-Chancellor, Frank Thistlethwaite, who was to be closely involved in the Sainsbury Centre project, declared that 'the name Sainsbury will stand alongside those who have created the great centres of art in British universities from the seventeenth to the present century: Ashmole at Oxford in 1677, Fitzwilliam at Cambridge in 1812, Courtauld at London in 1932 and now Sainsbury at East Anglia.'

However, the Sainsbury Centre was to be a new sort of art museum – a 'centre', significantly, not a gallery – very different in character from its precursors. Integration was to be a key theme. With the support of the University, it was proposed that in addition to gallery space the project should include teaching and library accommodation for what was then the School of Fine Art, to be funded under the auspices of the University Grants Committee. In due course, in discussion with the University (led by Thistlethwaite), a senior common room and a restaurant were added to the brief. Not everyone warmed to these radical notions. Some academics, Foster remembers, 'regarded it as absolutely outrageous that these two worlds

Left: Norman Foster has described the decision about where to site the Sainsbury Centre within the UEA campus as one of the most difficult aspects of the design process. As this sketch by Foster demonstrates, the site eventually chosen terminated the then major linear sequence of Sir Denys Lasdun's university buildings, where it enjoyed uninterrupted views of the surrounding countryside and the newly created lake, or 'broad'.

Left: An early drawing exploring options for the siting relative to the existing campus buildings.

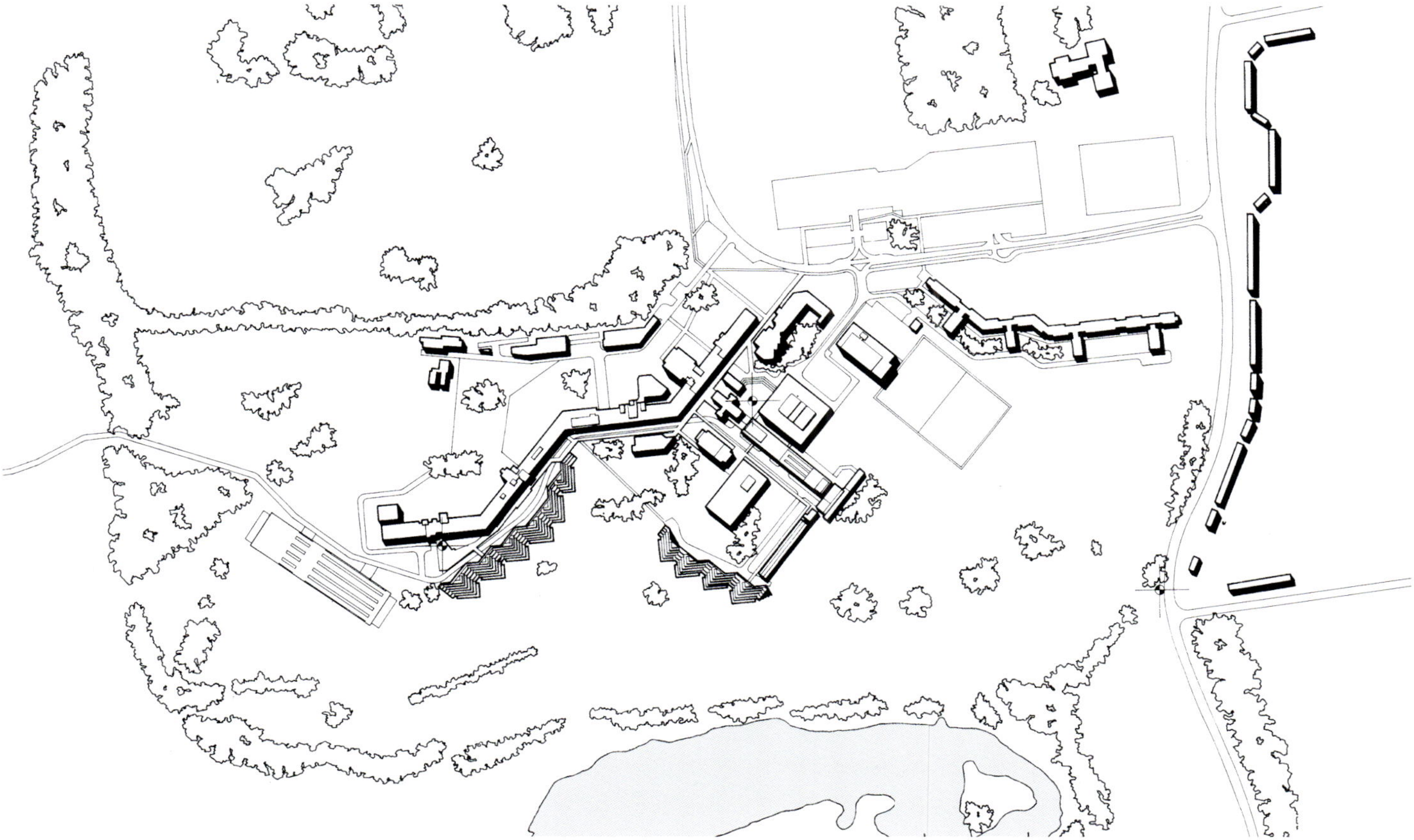

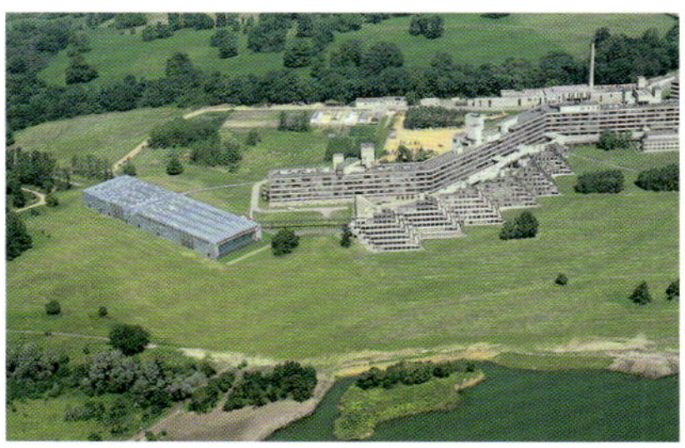

Left and above: The location, away from the other arts buildings and next to the scientists, accorded with the Sainsburys' intention that the building should fit in with the general life of the university; they did not want to encourage an 'arts ghetto' on the campus. Pragmatically, a road complete with services anticipated future development in that direction; with a fixed budget, this had the benefit of releasing the maximum funds for the building itself.

Below left: While the final location of the building was being decided, the design concept of a single building was also evolving. A portal-frame structure provided the clear span that Norman Foster desired for the building. Early models explored a range of engineering and cladding solutions to this basic form, with the cladding respectively located within or on top of the frame.

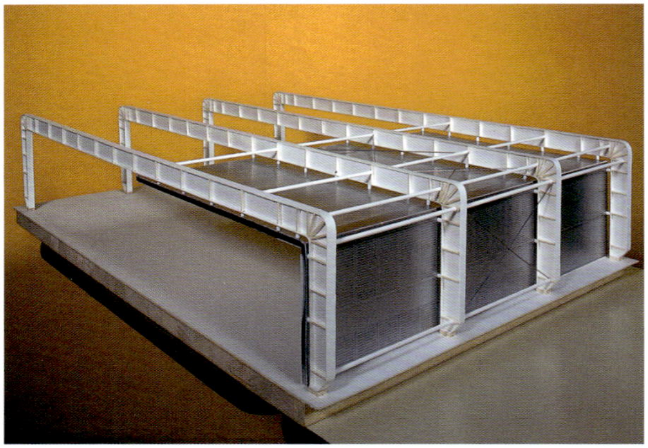

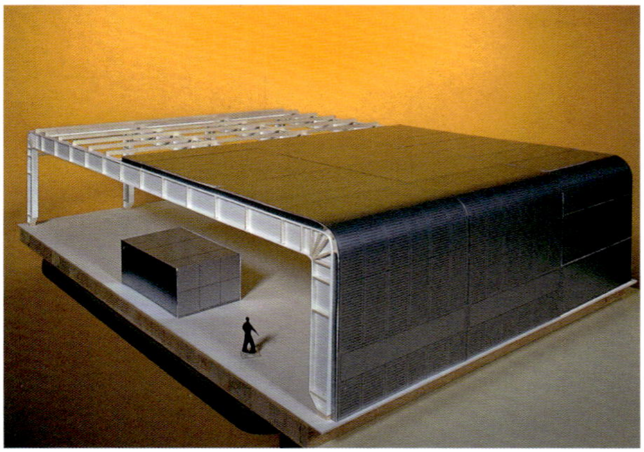

would come together and that you would be able to teach in an informal manner amongst works of art.' Given these objections (which focused on issues of noise and security), the logical conclusion, would to have been to design not one, but two or even three linked pavilions – an idea that, with the support of Thistlethwaite, was quickly dismissed. As the design developed, and academic concerns continued to be voiced, Foster would have to take on the often difficult role of intermediary with the university community.

The theme of integration was reflected equally in the multi-disciplinary – and youthful – team that Foster brought together to develop the project. A key team member was the structural engineer Anthony Hunt, who had worked with Norman and Wendy Foster at Team 4 on the house at Creek Vean and the Reliance Controls Electronics Factory, and had been involved in all of Foster Associates' early projects. Quantity surveyor John Walker, a member of the Hanscomb Partnership, was another seasoned collaborator quickly brought on board. The Sainsburys nominated the distinguished garden designer Lanning Roper to handle the landscape aspects of the project.

The team within Foster Associates included, alongside Norman and Wendy Foster, Loren Butt (who had trained as a services engineer and worked with

Right: The initial solution for the structure was a 300mm-deep steel portal frame, which supported a secondary system of pressed aluminium sections and 75mm-thick insulated panels. Bolted together to form a matrix, the substructure incorporated lighting, acoustic panels and services.

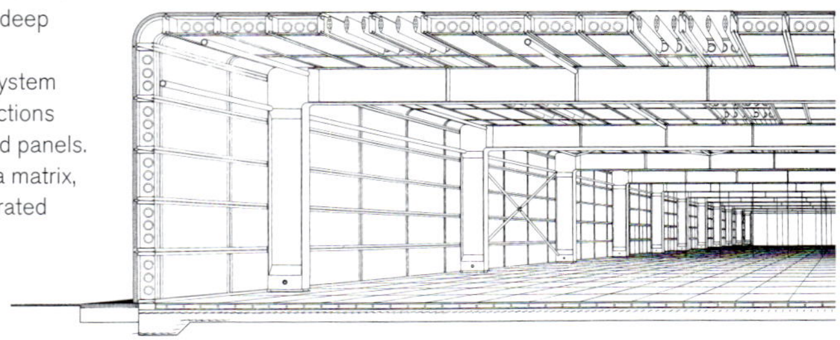

Right: An early model of the portal-frame structure proposal.

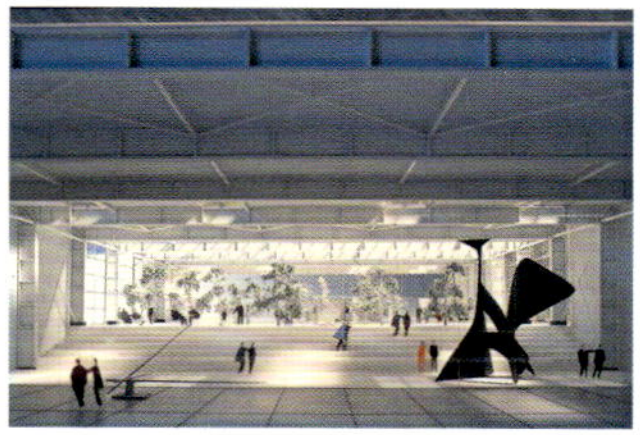

Foster on the Fred Olsen project before joining the practice), Arthur Branthwaite, Chubby Chhabra, Spencer de Grey (then a recent recruit, who would work on presentation drawings), Roy Fleetwood, Birkin Haward, Richard Horden, Tomm Nyhuus, Tony Pritchard, Ian Ritchie, and Bodo Zapp; they would be joined by David Nelson in 1976. Soon after his appointment was confirmed, Foster took members of the team to meet the Sainsburys at Smith Square.

Teamwork was, as with all Foster's projects, fundamental to the success of the Sainsbury Centre – 'it was the integration of the different disciplines that produced an integrated building,' recalls Loren Butt, while Birkin Haward remembers 'the seamless, holistic experience of dealing with a real client, not a committee.'

The Sainsburys' vision of an informal, enjoyable learning environment, with a domestic ambience, owes something, perhaps, to Kettle's Yard in Cambridge, created by Jim Ede from 1956 onwards, where works of art are displayed in an essentially domestic setting. But Kettle's Yard was largely a conversion of a group of old houses (an extension was added by Leslie Martin in 1970). A new museum of the post-war era, which had impressed Foster when he visited it as a student, was the Louisiana Museum in Denmark, opened in 1958. It was the sense of intimacy in its galleries that Foster particularly liked; he equally admired the social mix it encouraged: '... everybody was there, young and old; everybody was enjoying it. Somehow you had this incredible feeling of vitality and exuberance.'

The only feature of the Louisiana Museum that seemed deficient was security – 'you almost felt that with a screwdriver you could have opened the whole place up and taken whatever was in storage away.' There was no dedicated zone for the delivery and reception of works of art – a naive omission, Foster felt. Louisiana was on the list of art museums which Norman and Wendy Foster and the Sainsburys visited as they refined the brief for the UEA project. In October 1974 they went to Louisiana, to Mies van der Rohe's New National Gallery in Berlin – completed just six years earlier and Mies' last great work – and to Aalto's gallery at Aalborg, in Jutland, where the magical quality of natural light within the building captivated Foster.

The point of the visits, 'a research marathon' in Foster's words, was not only to enjoy the formal aesthetics of these buildings but equally to discover how they worked – in terms of visitor facilities, storage, servicing, security, workshop provision and the rest. Foster later summarised the conclusions drawn from

Right: Structural engineer Anthony Hunt's exploratory drawings of the portal-frame solution show a considered resolution of the foot and 'angle' details together with fixing points for the tubular steel connecting rods and cross-bracing elements.

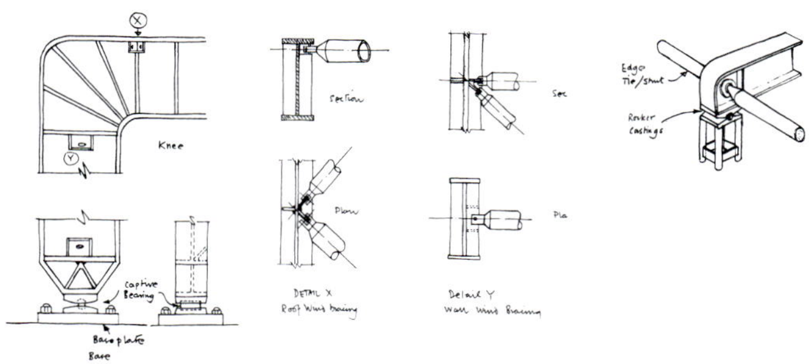

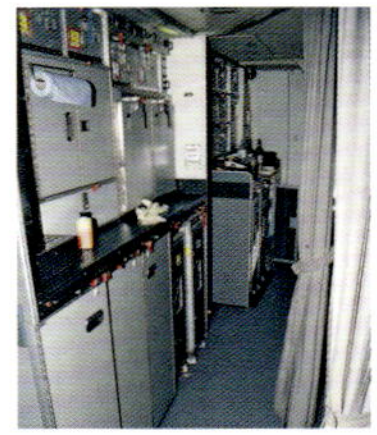

Right: In designing the service spaces, the design team sought the operational efficiency of the galleys within a Boeing 747.

this marathon: 'an awareness of the positive qualities of tuneable natural top light; the importance of flexibility for change and growth; the need for effective but not labour-intensive security; the value of usable storage space – most museums seemed to have as many works of art closeted away inaccessibly as on display; the need to service a gallery without disturbing either exhibits or users – changing and adjusting lamps and air filters, for example; a desire to respect and integrate social elements; and a need to understand the furniture and installation of exhibits as integrated elements of the design.'

The Sainsburys, Foster recalls, threw all their energies into the visits – which were followed by long evenings of discussion and debate. 'At times, Wendy and I struggled to keep up with them', he says. 'Throughout the project, they were tough, demanding, questioning – but they were never anything less than a fundamental part of the team.' Foster was amused to discover much later that the Sainsburys had confided to friends that the pace set by Norman and Wendy on the trip had been incredibly hard to maintain.

Foster and the Sainsburys had agreed on the character of the building they were setting out to create – it was to be a place, in Robert Sainsbury's words, 'in which people could relax, look at works of

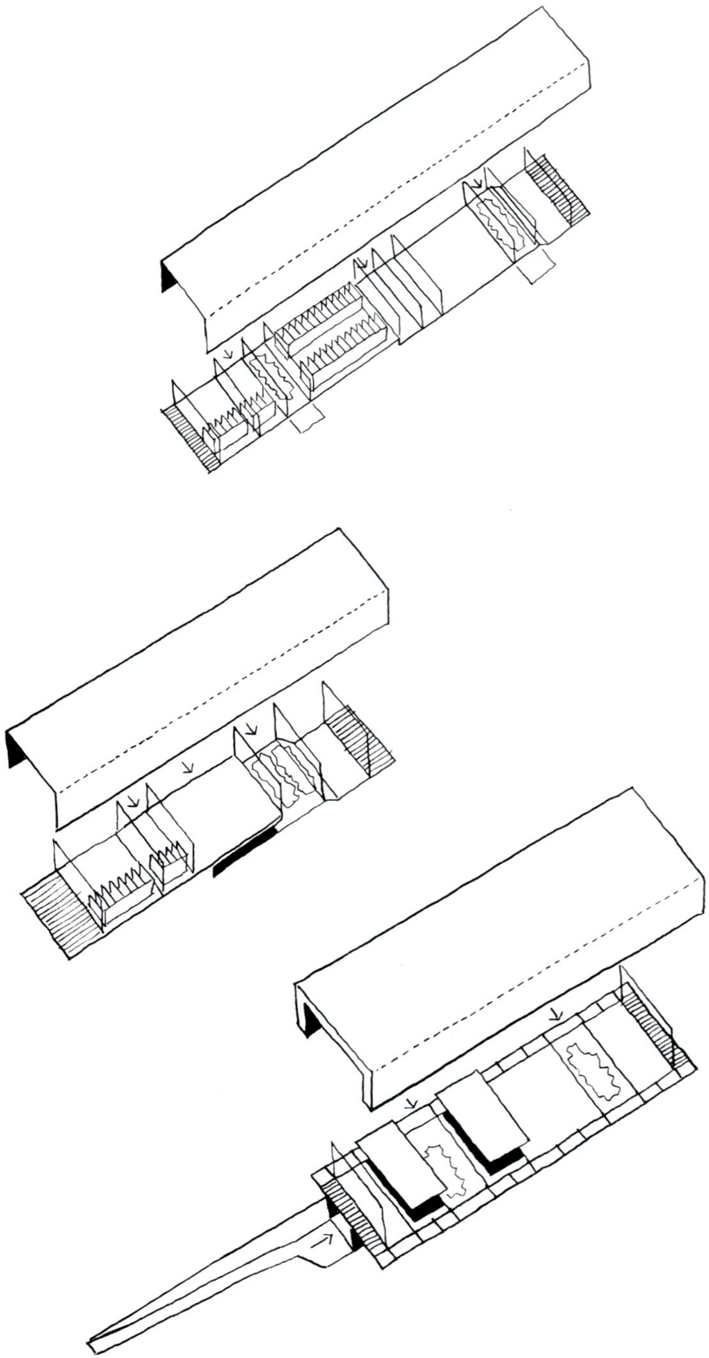

Left: The process of resolving the subdivision of spaces, and where to house the services installations within the building, was to lead to the adoption of a basement 'undercroft' and the 'double-skin' system, which is explained in these sketches by Norman Foster.

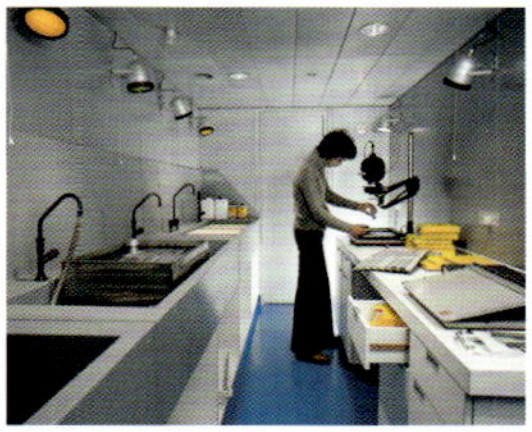

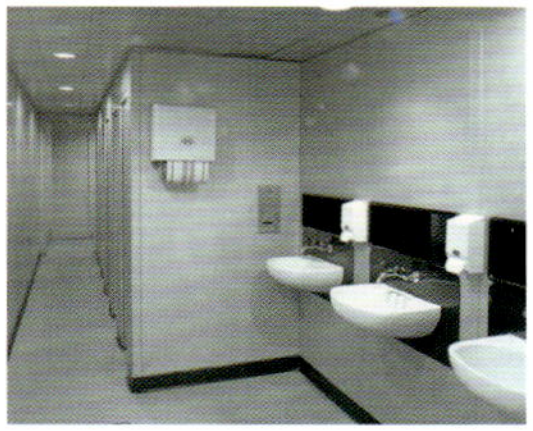

Far left, left: A photographic darkroom and lavatories are located within the building's 2.4-metre deep wall zone.

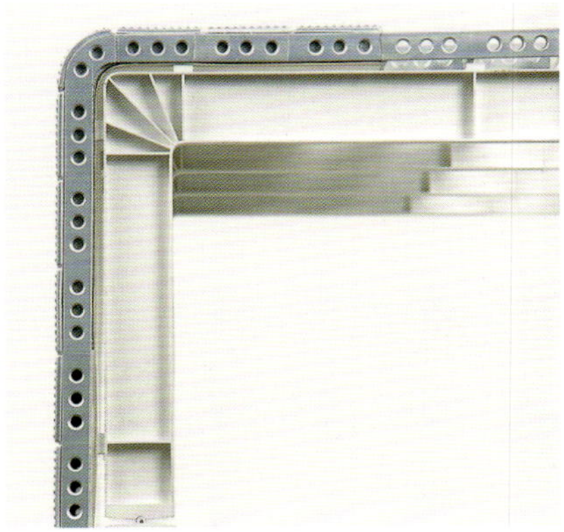

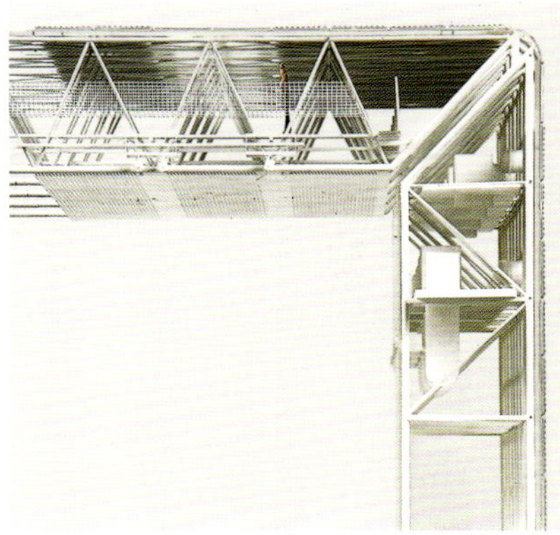

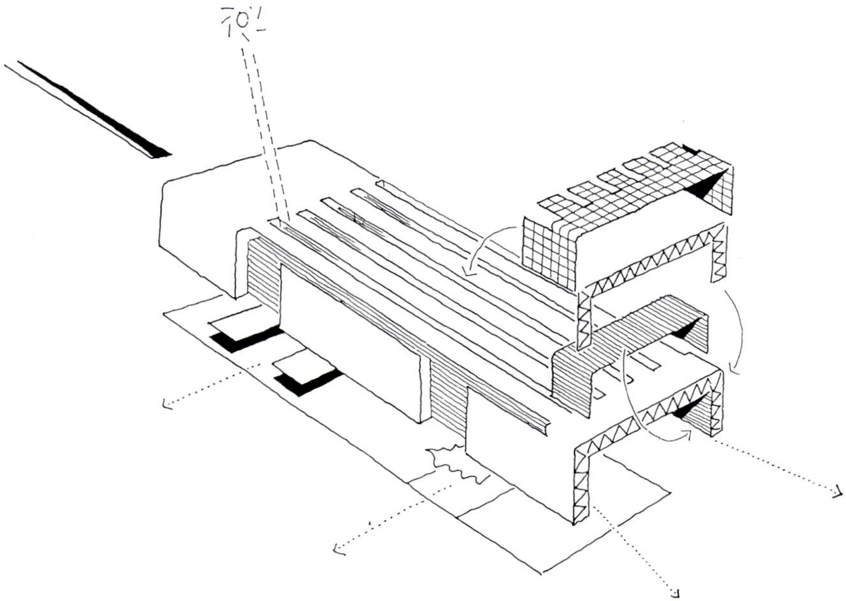

art in a leisurely manner if they so wished, work, read a novel or just dream away.' But the written brief, in so far as there was one, was entirely non-prescriptive in terms of the form of the building. 'Norman's brief was to give substance to a somewhat ill-defined concept,' Robert Sainsbury recalled in 1983. Foster remembers at one point presenting the Sainsburys with numerous possible options and Lisa saying: 'Norman, don't take us through the whole presentation, just tell us what you want to do.'

The decision having been taken that all the elements in the project – art gallery, teaching, library and other academic facilities, and public spaces – should be accommodated within one building on the selected site led to the concept, seen in Foster's earliest sketches, of a longitudinal container, initially with a series of compartments within it – storage and other cellular private spaces had to be provided within the envelope.

If it was the Fred Olsen Amenity Centre that had attracted the attention of the Sainsburys, it is another Foster project, the warehouse and offices for Modern Art Glass at Thamesmead, completed in 1973, that offers a more obvious antecedent of the Sainsbury Centre design at this point. Modern Art Glass was clad in corrugated metal, supported on a portal frame, with

Above right: A breakthrough came with the change from a single-skin wall to a double-layered solution, with a 2.4-metre deep structure, which could absorb the many small cellular spaces required. In these comparative models the advantages of the deep-wall scheme are apparent.

Right: Norman Foster's explanatory diagram of the final scheme shows how the structural and cladding elements come together.

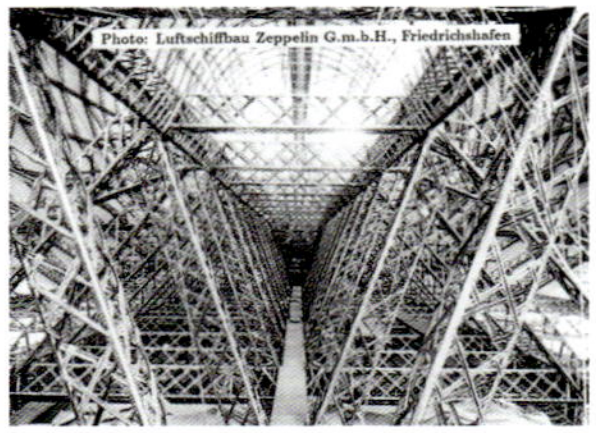

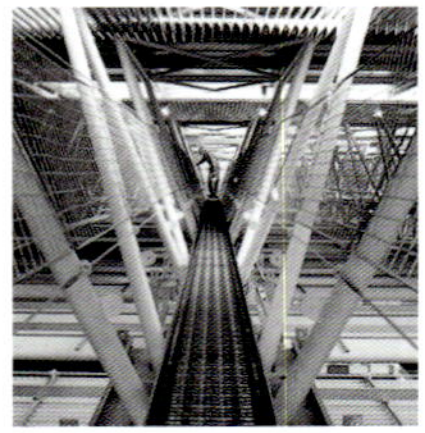

Far left and left: The service catwalk within the depth of the Sainsbury Centre's roof structure compared with the service gangway of the airship Graf Zeppelin: structural lightness is a pervasive theme.

its walls and roof formed in 'wrap-around' fashion, while the south elevation was a sheer wall of glazing. The SAPA factory at Tibshelf, also completed in 1973 – 'about as smooth and enigmatic a box as one could wish to see,' as the critic Alastair Best described it at the time – equally prefigured Foster's treatment of the Sainsbury Centre. (The Sainsbury Centre itself, Best wrote later, was 'the last word in sleek sheds'.)

The idea of an all-enveloping container along the lines of Modern Art Glass or SAPA offered the potential for achieving the qualities of openness and flexibility that architect and client saw as fundamental to the project. However, providing for the variety of uses and activities which the container was to house threatened to destroy its essential clarity – a secure loading bay area for works of art, for example, would have to be provided, linked to storage and workshop spaces. There was equally the issue of how the service spaces – such as lavatories, darkrooms and other technical facilities – were to be accommodated. 'It was one of the classic challenges in modern architecture,' says Foster, 'how to handle the relationship between free, flexible space and the fixed service elements.'

One element in the scheme with considerable implications for the future – and a breakthrough in the design process – was the decision to create a basement level beneath the 'shed'. This took the form of a spinal corridor extending the full length of the building, serving storage and workshop areas and accessible from the gallery level at strategic points by stairs and service lifts. A secure loading bay at basement level, connected to the main service road on the campus, provided for the safe delivery of works of art and other material. Significantly, the basement would allow the design team to dispense with some of the potential intrusions into the shed. Later it would open the way for the expansion of the Centre with the creation of the Crescent Wing, though this was not foreseen at the time.

Equally, of course, this arrangement can be seen as a precedent for Foster's terminal building at Stansted Airport. There, the basement – or 'undercroft' – houses all the heating, ventilating and other plant usually located at roof level, thus liberating the roof canopy to flood the concourse with daylight.

The strategy of containing the teaching and library spaces for the School of Fine Art within freestanding and structurally independent 'buildings within a building' also solved a number of problems. These elements were topped by mezzanine levels (one housing the senior common room), but were kept low enough to maintain the long vista through the great

Right: In this early sketch Norman Foster anticipates an inner lining of louvres and the location of service plant within the structural double-skin. However, no structural form is yet suggested.

The crucial decision, taken 'at five minutes to midnight', to change to a double-skin system allowed us complete spatial freedom. It meant that all the services could be hidden within the depth of the walls and roof.
Norman Foster, 2010

room. Nonetheless, one challenge remained: the services. Heating was to be supplied to the building from the university's district heating system, so no boiler room was required, but how would it be ventilated and kept cool? It seemed inevitable that the walls and roof would have to accommodate electrical and mechanical plant. The proposed structural system, a 300mm-deep steel portal frame, with insulated cladding panels bolted to an aluminium subframe, allowed little scope for concealing services or providing a discreet location for those facilities that had to be placed at ground floor level. 'The prospect was one of ducts everywhere', says Loren Butt.

Foster was unhappy with the portal-frame solution. The team had debated a number of possible strategies for resolving the issue, but there was a crucial moment in September 1975 when things came to a head. Foster compares it to the eleventh-hour decision to substitute a great arch for the original masted roof structure planned for Wembley Stadium. Norman, Wendy, Tony Hunt and others were sitting around the circular table in Foster Associates' Fitzroy Street office. 'Norman said: "We need to rethink it – it needs to be a double-skin structure."' Hunt recalls; 'It was incredibly late in the day – all the drawings had been done and we were about to go to tender for the main structure.'

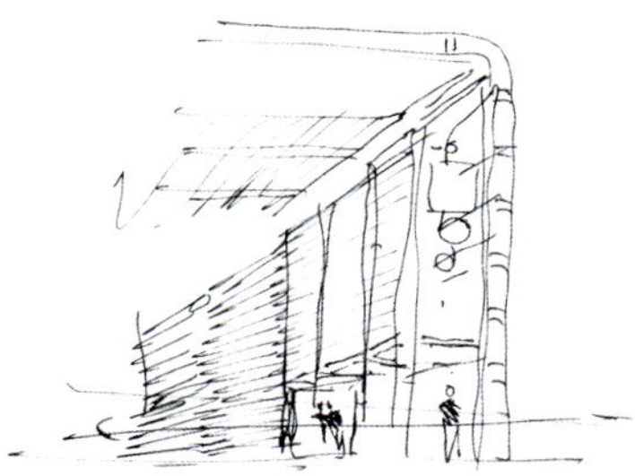

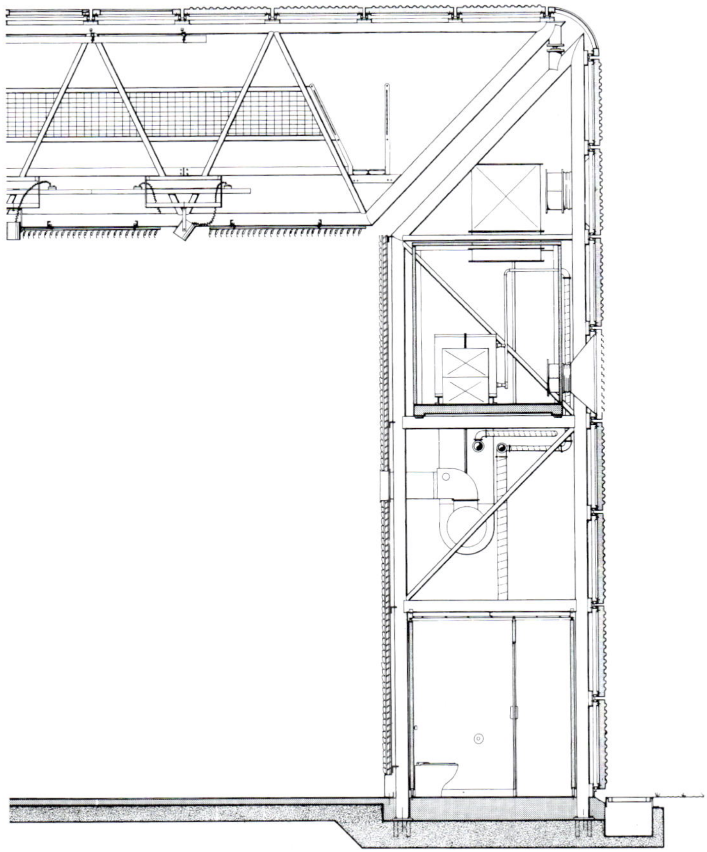

Above: The 2.4-metre depth of the truss structure conceals services and back-up facilities in the wall zone and provides access to gallery lighting within the roof. General service rooms – including WCs and stores – are at ground level; above are runs of pipes and ducts, with mechanical plant at the upper level.

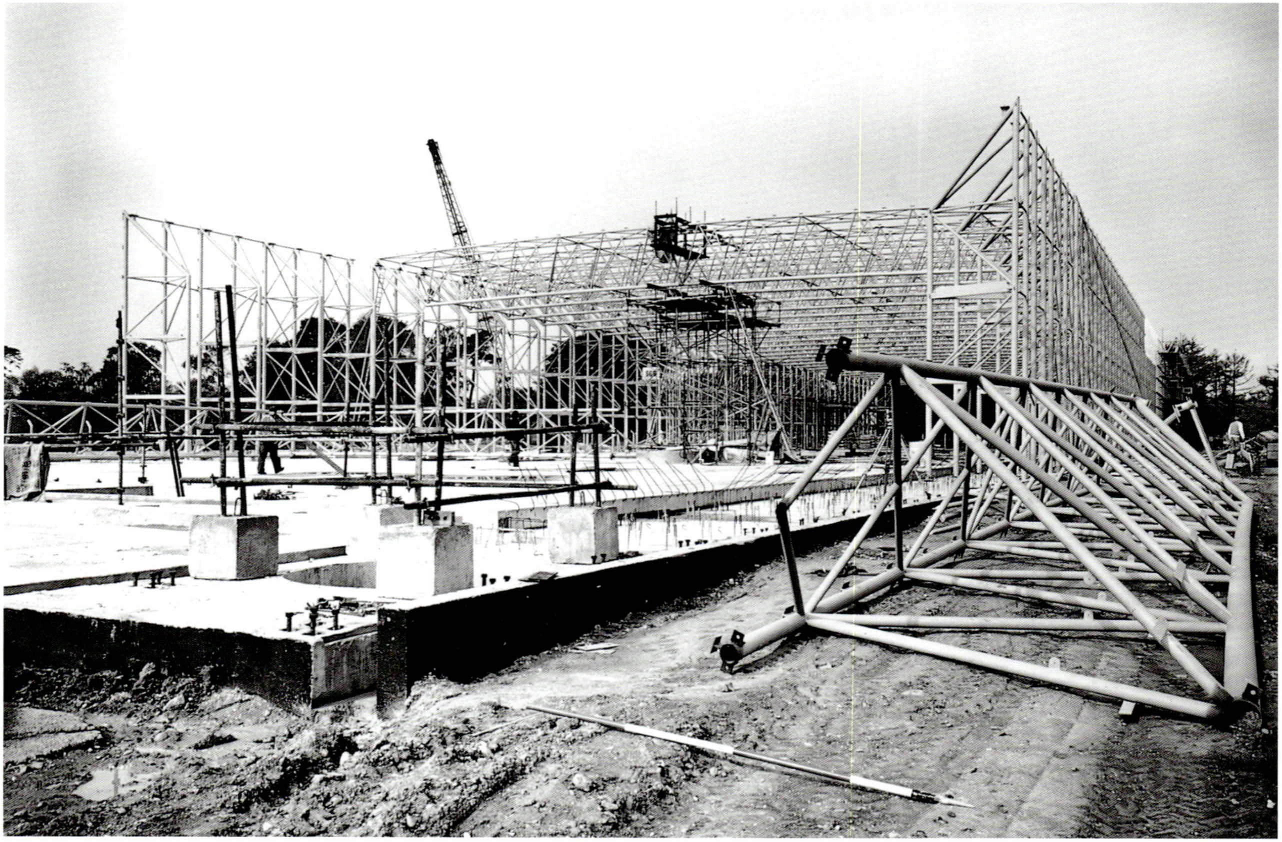

Above: The concrete basement and ground slab were the only parts of the building that required intensive site construction. The majority of the components were prefabricated elsewhere and assembled on site.

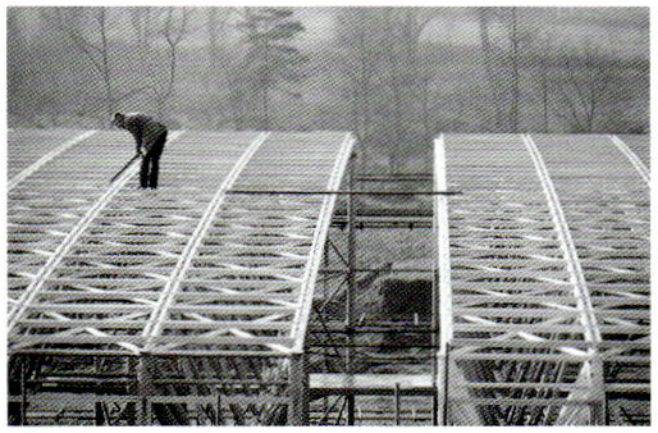

Left: The structural trusses and towers were prefabricated at the Tubeworkers factory in Warwickshire and arrived on site complete with their final coat of paint. Only the roof trusses required final welding as, due to their size, they had to be transported in two sections.

The team set to work immediately to realise the alternative structural solution. A Triodetic system – a form of space-frame – was briefly considered but rejected. The answer was a truss structure with an open framework, supporting a double-skin whose 2.4-metre depth would provide space for services and secondary functions, thereby leaving the primary spaces uncluttered. The adoption of this double wall would, as Foster predicted, allow the creation of the sublime shed that he had imagined from the start. It also had important environmental benefits, shielding the interior from solar gain and reducing the energy required to heat or cool the main space.

Tony Hunt developed the structural concept into what was eventually built – a system of triangular vertical trusses or columns, with corresponding trussed beams spanning 35 metres to form the roof. Dimensionally, the trusses were set at 1.8 metres wide to accommodate the cladding panels. These had already been designed as a bespoke system, with Tony Pritchard as the team member in charge, and were in the process of being fabricated. The trusses are designed to sit on concrete pad foundations so there was no need for deep piling.

Individual truss members are made of welded steel tubing and vertical and horizontal members are connected by a pin joint on one side and a slip joint on the other, an arrangement that eliminates the need to thicken the structure at the junction. In essence, this is a simple post-and-beam system, with no secondary structural elements, but it provides the necessary strength and rigidity using remarkably minimal means. To stiffen the structure further, the last two trusses at each end are welded together to form a box truss.

Tony Hunt recalls Foster's insistence that the junction between walls and roof should be curved, not formed as a right angle. It meant some deft calculations to find a way of offsetting the structural load. To aid rainwater run-off, and to counteract the illusion of sag frequently perceived in large horizontal spans, the roof trusses are constructed with a slight entasis, arcing upwards 150mm from the ends to the centre point. 'The tolerances were very tight,' Hunt says, 'but once the steelwork was delivered to site it went together perfectly – just like a Meccano kit.'

The glazed end elevations, which are set back to reveal the truss structure, were equally the subject of extended study and discussion. The aim was to create transparent walls, with as little structure as possible.

At Willis Faber, the glazing had been hung from the top of the building. The structural system at the Sainsbury Centre did not allow a repeat of this strategy

Right: The cladding panels are sealed by a neoprene lattice gasket, seen here draped over the roof of the building during construction. The lattice arrived in manageable 'ladder' sections, which were joined on site to form the largest continuous neoprene net in the world.

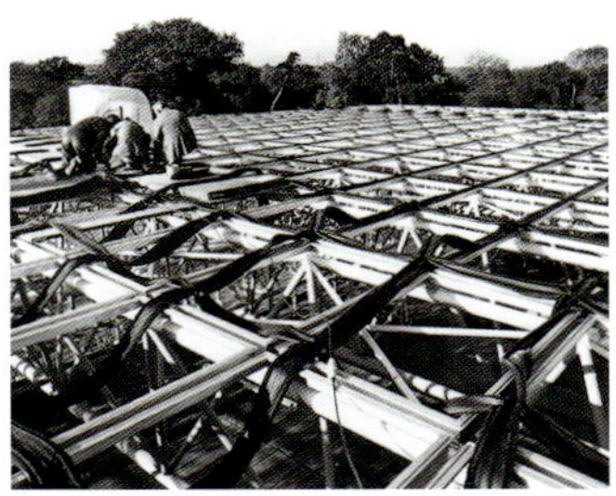

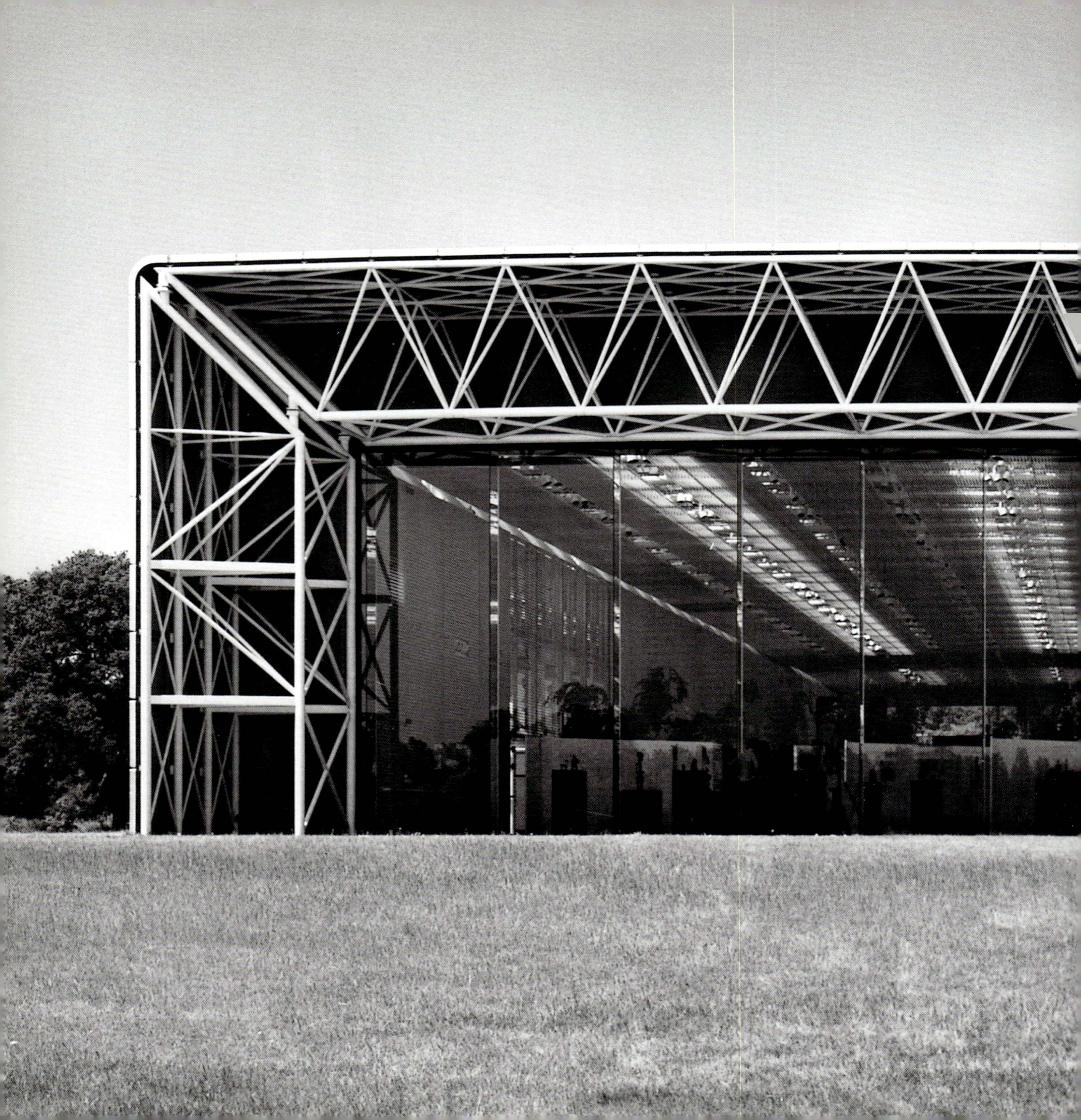

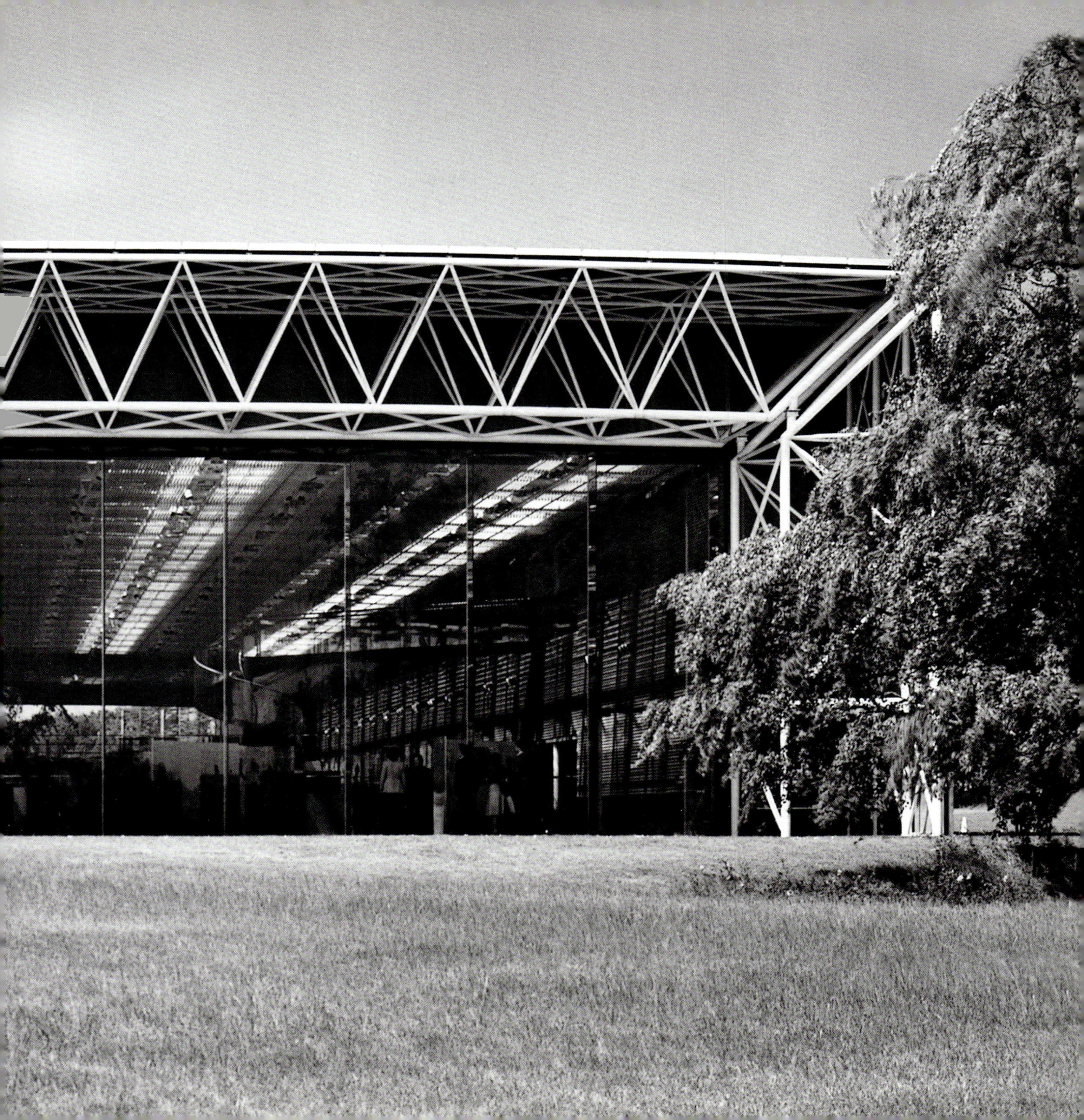

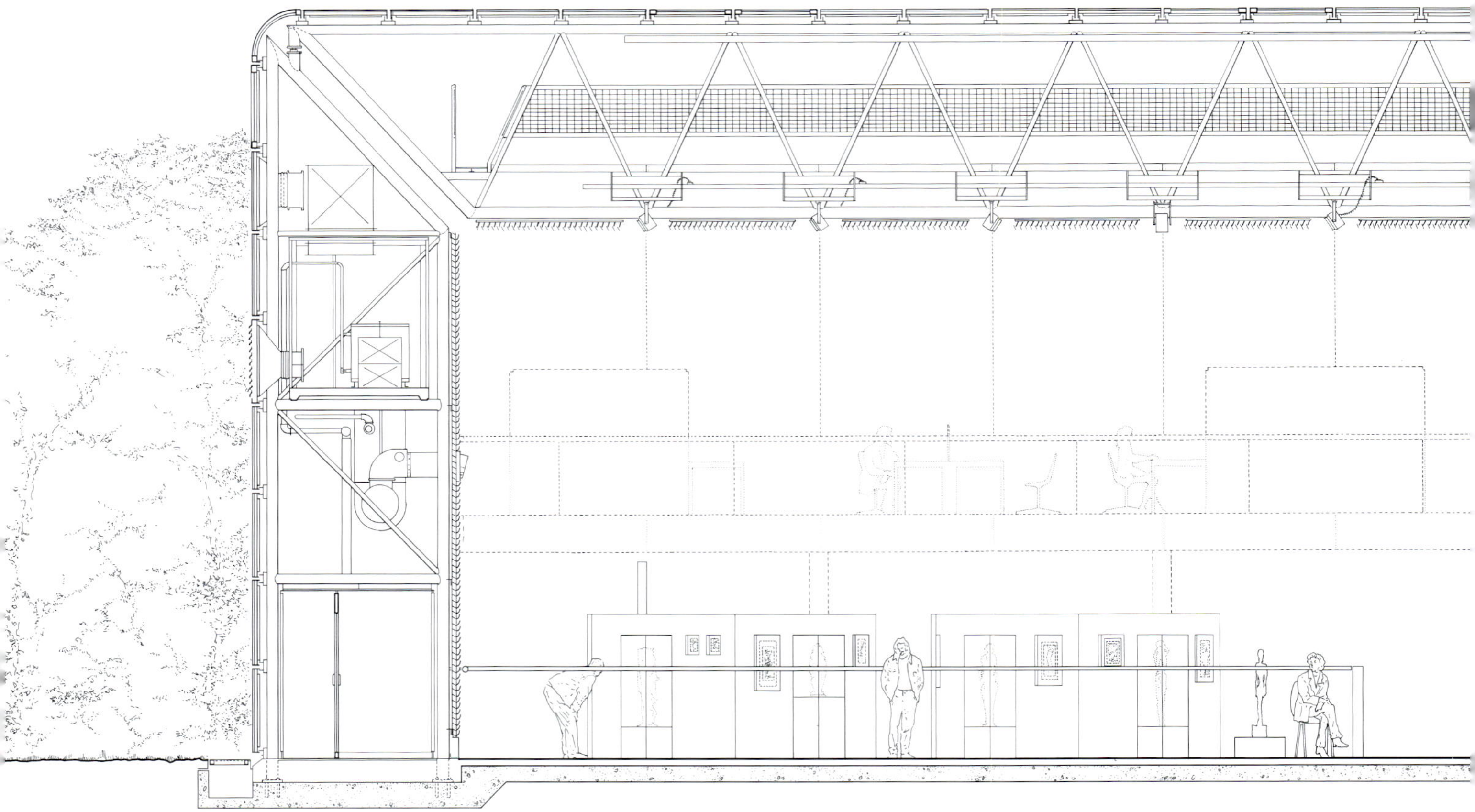

Previous pages: The Sainsbury Centre seen shortly after it opened in 1978; looking into the temporary exhibitions gallery from the lawn.

Above: A cross-section through the building as modified in 2006, looking from the temporary exhibitions gallery through to the 'living area'. The undercroft, which originally contained technical areas, now also contains a bookshop and provides a covered link to the Crescent Wing.

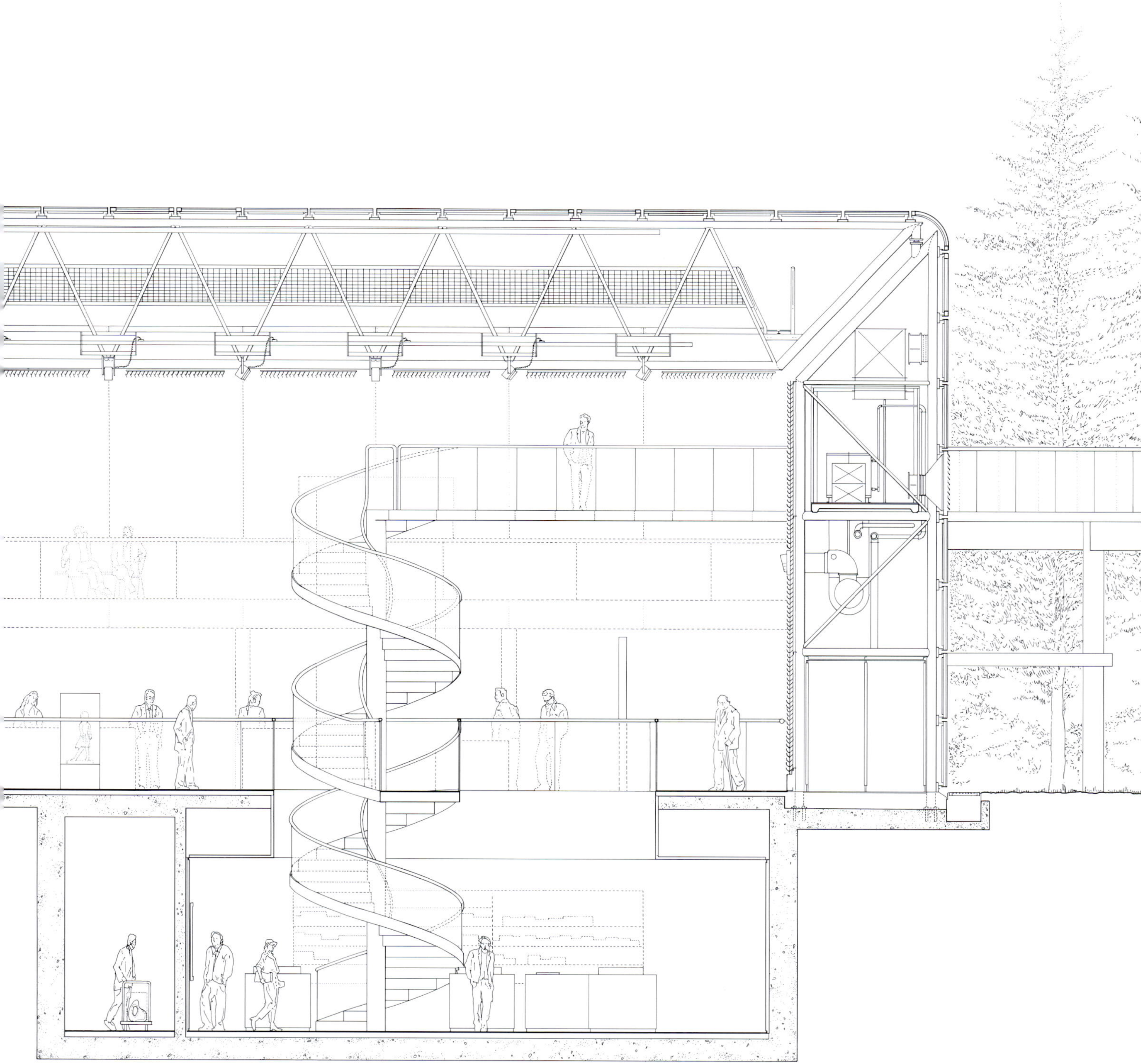

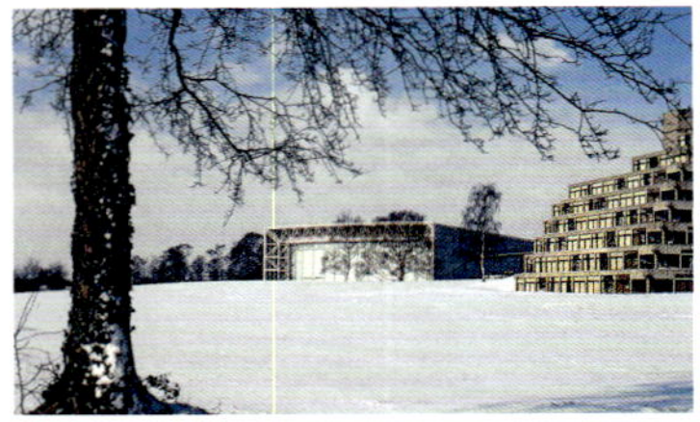

Right: The building seen in deep snow in 1978; sunlight is reflected off the blinds in the temporary exhibitions gallery.

and the use of vertical glass mullions or fins to support the huge sheets of glass (there are no horizontal transoms) was a daring solution which provided the requisite degree of transparency.

When the decision was taken to start afresh, it fell to Foster to inform the Sainsburys and gain their approval. Fortunately, as he recalls, 'Bob and Lisa recognised immediately that this was the right direction – there was never any question of them being anything but completely supportive.'

The built solution has that sense of inevitability that attaches to all great works of engineering or architecture; even though the route that led to it may not have been straightforward, it just feels 'right'. As Foster has written, 'The visual dimension of a structure is also its spiritual dimension ... how it will look and how it will work become conceptually inseparable through the process of design'.

The change of design direction was handled swiftly, and while there was a minor delay to the schedule, there was no significant increase in cost. The original intention had been to begin construction in the autumn of 1975. In fact, the contractor, RG Carter, took possession of the site in the first week of January 1976 and began work on the basement and concrete raft that forms the floor of the Centre. These were the only parts of the building that relied on wet trades, being formed of reinforced in-situ concrete. While this first phase of work was in progress, the tubular steel trusses and towers were being fabricated at Tubeworkers' factory in Warwickshire. Tony Hunt worked closely with the Tubeworkers team, led by John Hirst, on the detailed design of the structure, an example of the way in which Foster's collaborative approach to working with industry was to transform the world of construction.

The steel trusses were delivered to site ready painted for assembly. Only the roof sections were too long to be transported in one piece and had to be fabricated in two parts and welded together on site.

In the tradition of Joseph Paxton's Crystal Palace, the Centre was 'assembled' rather than 'built'. 'The building is essentially a series of machine-made components and that relates to the realities of cost control, to the manner in which buildings are assembled, and the materials from which they are made,' Norman Foster told an audience at UEA, shortly before the Centre opened on 7 April 1978.

That theme was taken up again a few weeks later, when Foster flew Buckminster Fuller down to UEA in the helicopter for a tour of the Centre. Fuller (1895-1983), the visionary American inventor and designer,

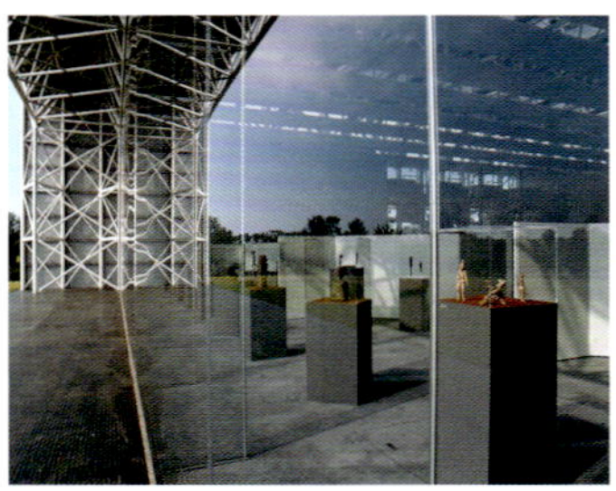

Left: Looking into the temporary exhibitions gallery from the loggia: transparency is another pervasive theme.

This shimmering structure of superplastic aluminium whistles past the grim cement grey of the University buildings like the Paris to Marseilles Mistral Express, immaculate in its pure green landscape. Stephen Gardiner, *The Listener*, February 1983

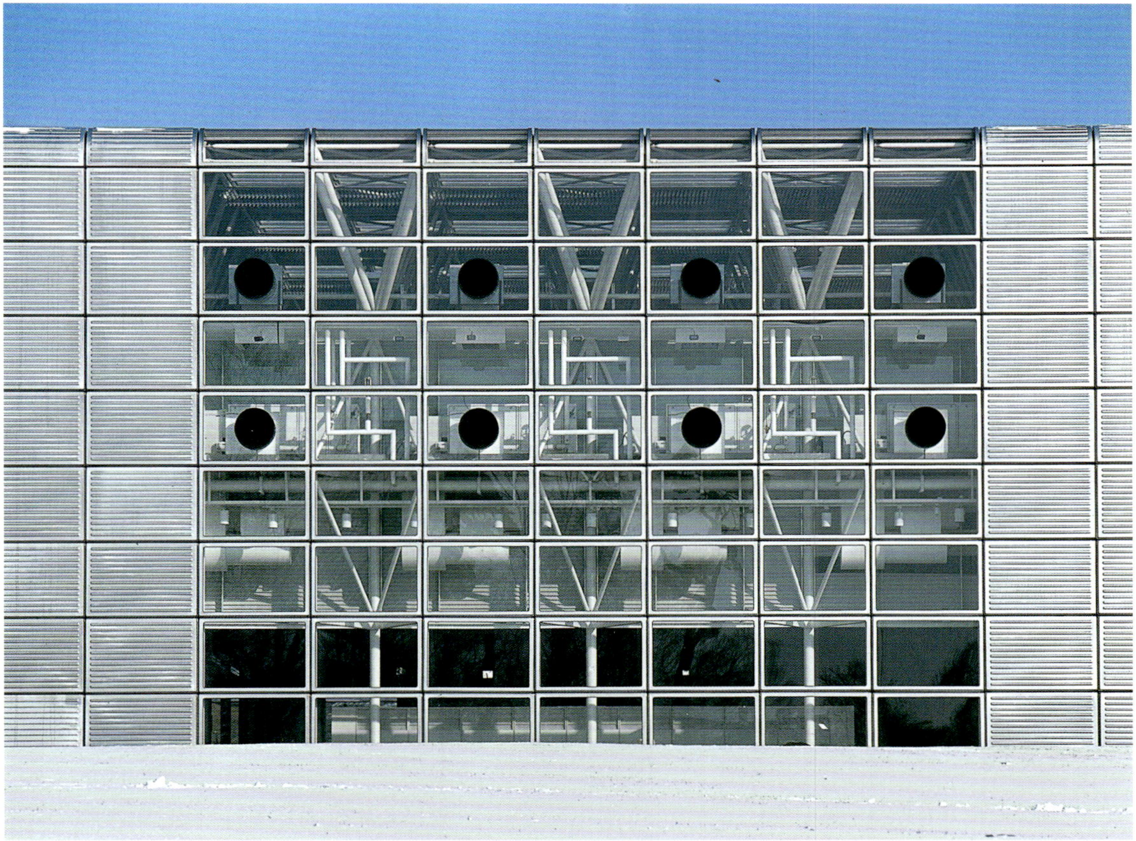

Above: One of the glazed sections that punctuate the length of the building. In this photograph, dating from 1978, the building has its original anodised aluminium cladding.

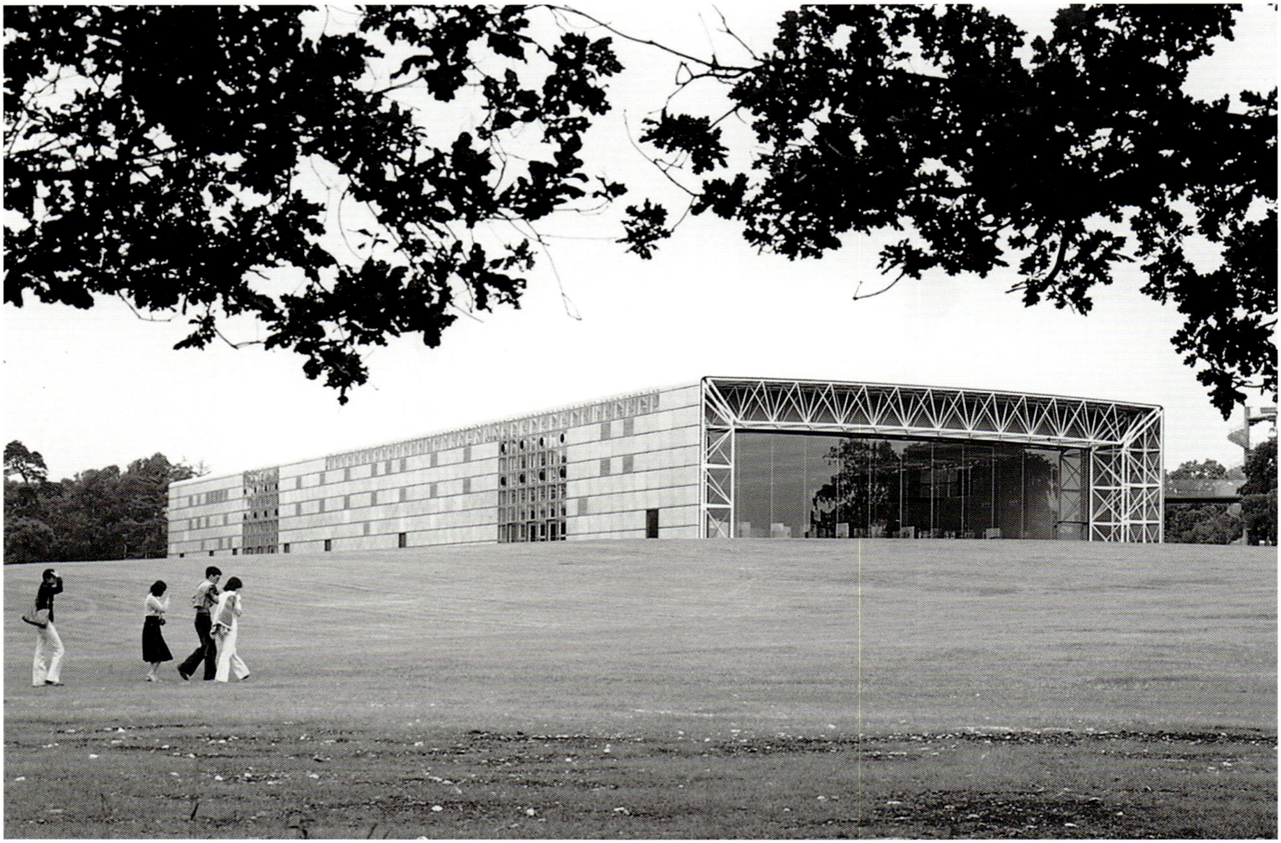

Above: The Sainsbury Centre seen from the banks of the broad, shortly after completion in 1978.

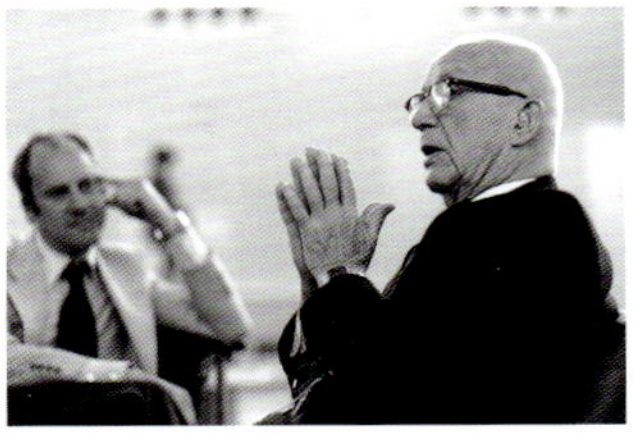

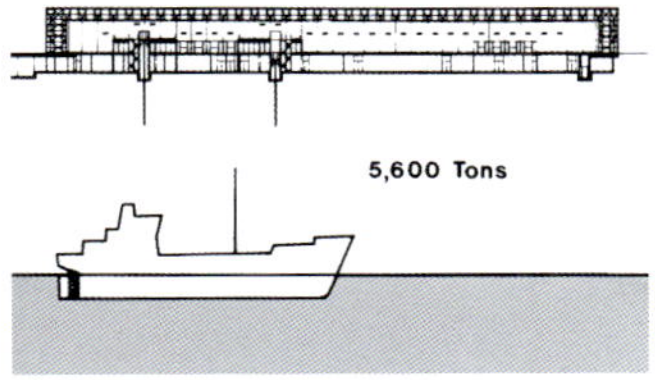

whom Foster had first met in 1971, was to become a potent influence on Foster's thinking. As they walked around the building, Fuller asked quite casually: 'How much does your building weigh, Norman?' 'Nobody in the team could answer the question straight away,' says Foster, 'but eventually we calculated that the building weighed precisely 5,618.6 tonnes. Interestingly, 4,500 tonnes of the total was accounted for by the basement, which encloses just 8 per cent of the volume of the main space but cost proportionally far more, took longer to construct, and has none of its visual delight.'

Years earlier, while still a partner in Team 4, Foster had concluded that the traditional 'wet' construction techniques employed in the early projects (the house at Creek Vean in Cornwall and the Murray Mews houses in London) represented a technological dead end. Team 4's Reliance Controls factory, completed in 1966, was an exercise in lightweight, steel-based construction, using prefabricated components. It was equally a pioneering example of what Foster calls 'the integrated enclosure', in which a single structure housed a number of functions normally articulated in separate containers.

At Reliance Controls – 'a democratic pavilion' – these included production and office areas and social spaces for both management and workers, who also shared a front door: something virtually unheard of in British industry in the 1960s.

The idea of the integrated enclosure informed Foster's unrealised Newport School project of 1967 and the IBM pilot head office at Cosham (1970-71). Just as managers and workers were brought under one roof at Reliance Controls, so at the Sainsbury Centre academics, students and members of the public (whether looking at art or enjoying lunch) share one big space – an 'urban room' as the critic Peter Buchanan has described it.

Norman Foster likens the arrangement to a railway carriage: 'You can connect all the spaces internally, so you can use the gallery as a short-cut to the school if you like. But you can also compartmentalise the spaces, just as you can close off the connections between one carriage and another. Each area is then private, secure and separate, because they may have different opening hours, or they may want to close one to do some kinds of work in private. You therefore have the option to open the thing up as a total entity, or close it off into a series of sealed areas.'

The layout of the interior of the main gallery – the 'living area' – was the subject of detailed and extended discussions with Robert and Lisa Sainsbury. Birkin Haward made freehand drawings, showing possible

Above: When Norman Foster took Buckminster Fuller around the Sainsbury Centre he posed the simple question: 'How much does your building weigh?' The answer was 5,618.6 tonnes, the superstructure accounting for just 20 per cent of the total.

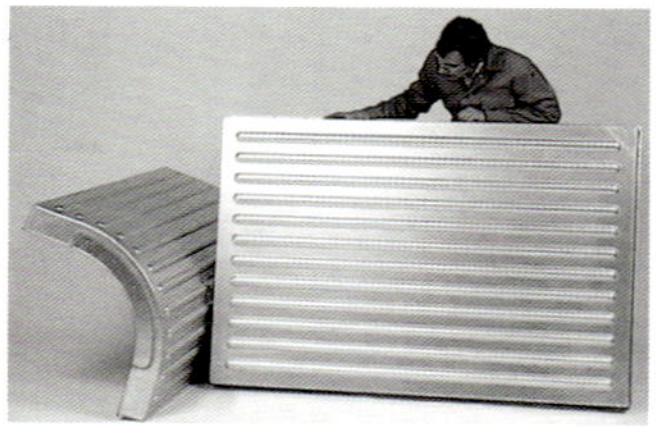

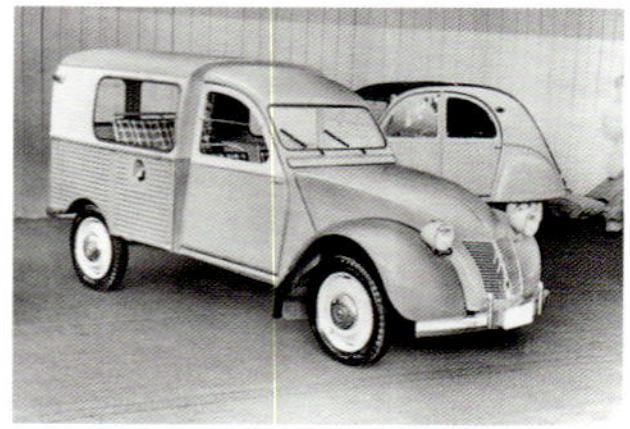

ways in which the space could be used. Scale models of the works of art were then made from cardboard, and team and clients looked at ways of arranging the exhibition.

Flexibility was as ever the key. No works were to be attached to the walls of the gallery. Instead the team devised a system of hinged panels (capable of being moved by two people) and display cases to evoke, as far as possible, the domestic scale of the spaces in which the works of art had long been seen. Display cases are of Perspex, set on 600mm-square plinths. The provision of informal seating was also considered vital to the concept of the gallery as a place where people might come to relax.

Looking back on the project when he introduced Norman Foster as the 1983 RIBA Royal Gold Medallist, Robert Sainsbury commented: 'There is an idea that small objects cannot be satisfactorily displayed in a tall building such as the Sainsbury Centre. I suggest that the height of the gallery is irrelevant … provided that, as at UEA, the space is a comfortable one to be in and the objects can be displayed at the right height for the average adult. The same argument can be applied to paintings and drawings, all of which are displayed at UEA on screens related to the human scale.'

The Sainsbury Centre and other Foster projects of the 1970s represented a vigorous response to a widely perceived crisis in British architecture – but the key to their revolutionary impact lies in their environmental performance as much their striking appearance. Designed at a time of rapidly rising energy costs and growing concern about the environmental impact of fossil fuel consumption, the Sainsbury Centre was envisaged from the beginning as a low-energy building with generous, though controlled, provision of daylight. Most new art galleries are air-conditioned sealed boxes but, as Foster reasoned, if the Sainsburys' collection had fared perfectly well for many years in their London house, in an ordinary domestic environment, why should the Sainsbury Centre be so different?

Daylight would be an essential feature of the galleries; and air conditioning was ruled out, except for specific areas, such as the workshops and storage spaces in the basement, where it was unavoidable. The form of the building, and in particular the generous floor to ceiling height (7.5 metres), encourages the free circulation of air. Fresh air is drawn into the building at low level, rises naturally as it warms and is expelled by extractors housed within the double skin. The high level of insulation in the cladding system is a further important factor in controlling temperatures within the

Above: The original aluminium cladding panels were ribbed, their profile echoing the treatment of the Citroën 2CV van.

Right: An exploded view of the structure and cladding assembly, showing the entire 'kit-of-parts'. The new cladding system consists of 1.8 x 1.2 metre white-painted aluminium panels with a smooth finish. Each panel fits into a net of neoprene gaskets which double as rainwater channels. There are five types of panel: flat panels are available in glazed, solid or grilled forms, while special glazed or solid panels turn the corner between wall and roof.

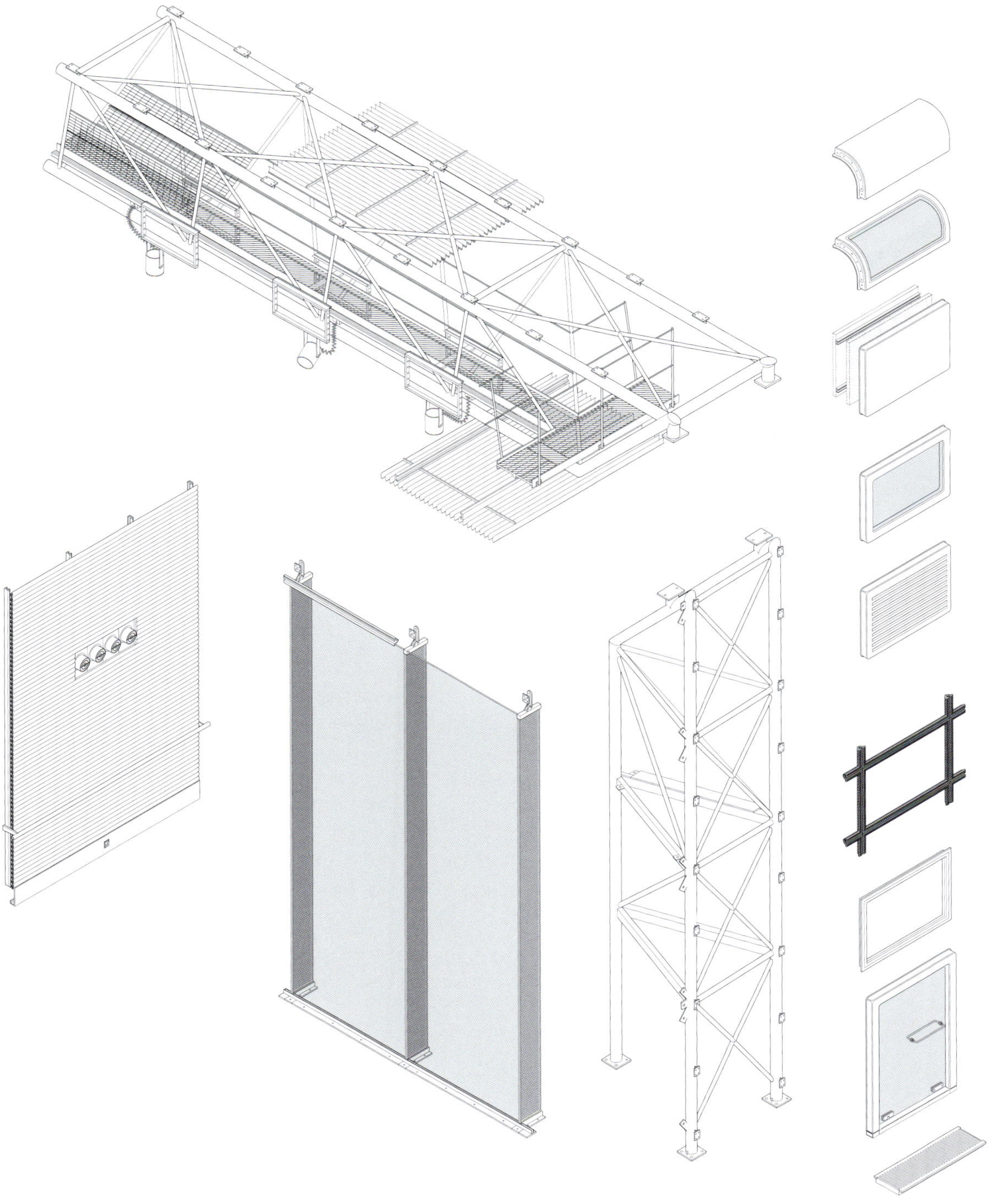

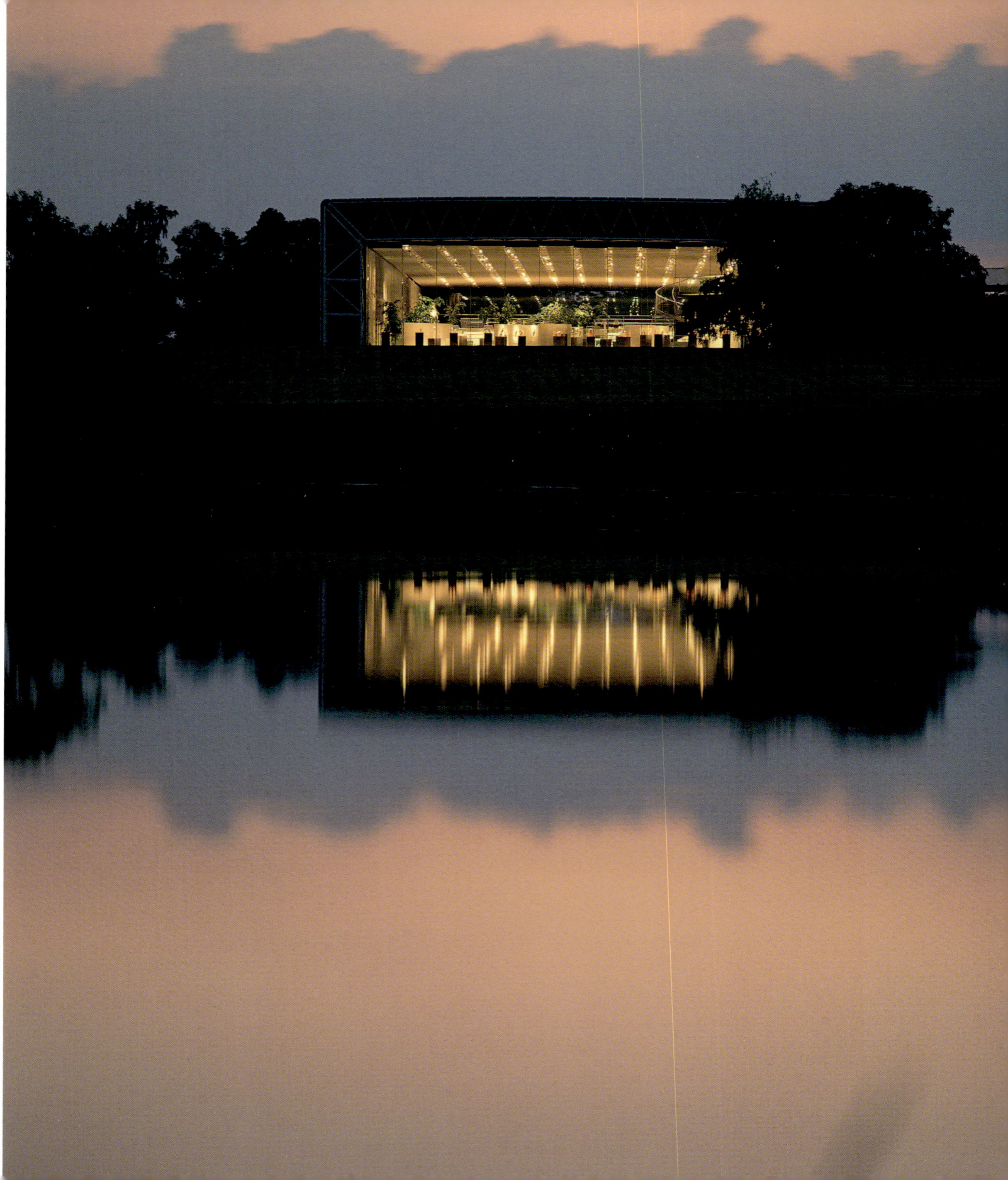

There isn't anyone in America who could do something as good as the Sainsbury Centre. England has at once become the leader in the engineering and technology game. Philip Johnson, lecture to the Architecture Club, 1979

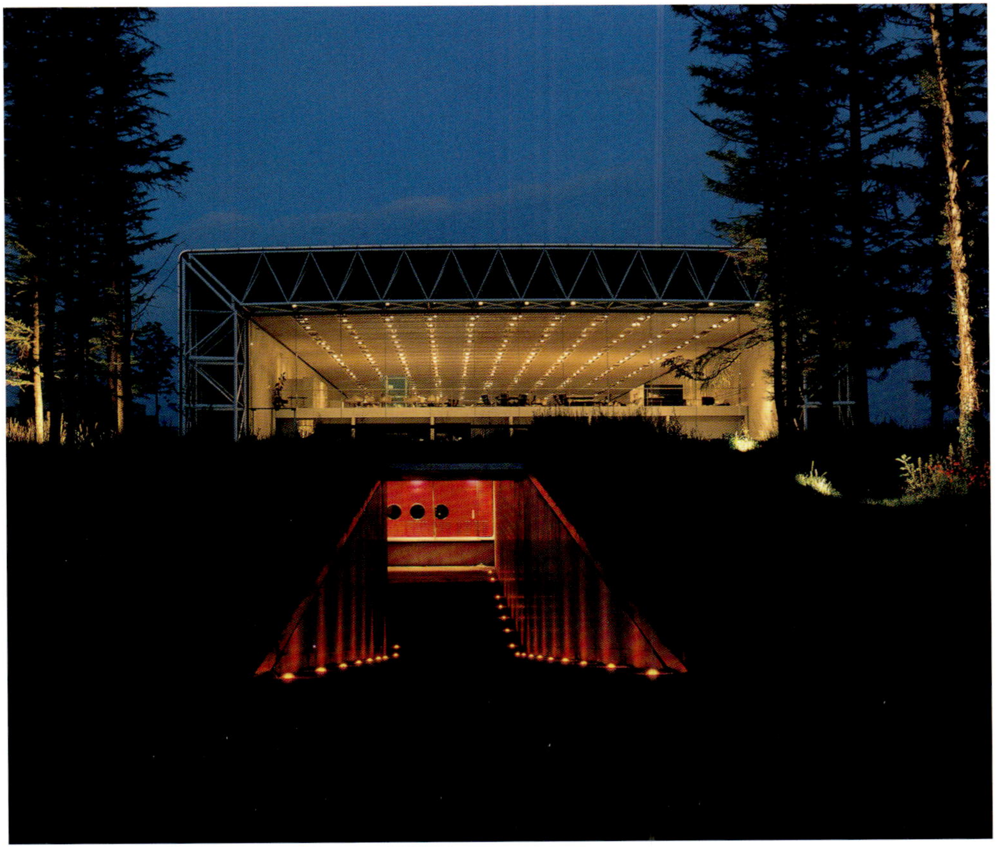

Left: As night falls, the Sainsbury Centre undergoes a dramatic transformation. It is seen here at dusk on completion, from across the lake or 'broad'.

Above: The delivery ramp emerges from the building's west end, but by using the natural contours of the site and the cover of trees for camouflage it remains invisible from the building itself. Concealed underground, the loading bays are provided with the best possible security.

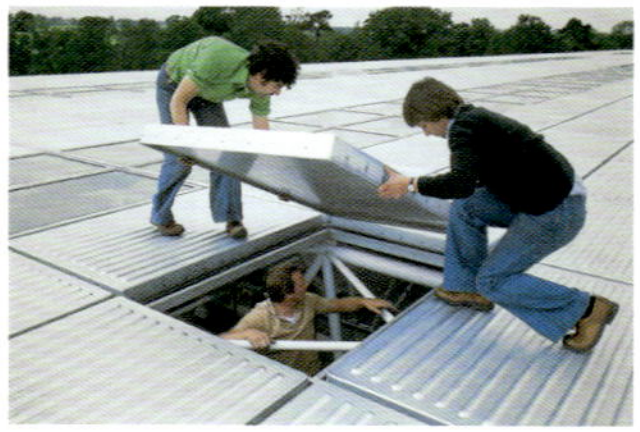

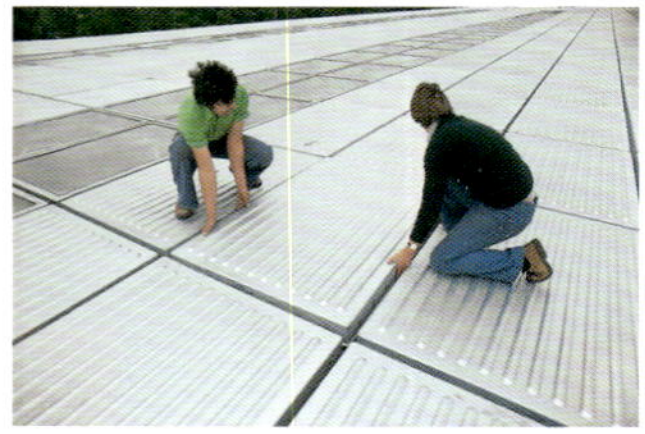

building. (Foster commented at the time that it was 'the kind of insulation you would normally associate with a cold store rather than anything to do with the building industry.')

The servicing solution, in which everything is accessible from behind the scenes, is designed to avoid some of the pitfalls seen in other art museums. There are no opening roof-lights which could leak, no water pipes in the gallery space, and a very simple drainage system. Nobody needs to bring in ladders to change a light bulb, and all the lighting can be accessed from the walkway in the roof space, where there is ample head height. A layer of fixed louvres lines the interior walls, with adjustable louvres – mechanically operated and linked to light sensors, but with manual override – installed in front of the glazed areas and across the ceiling. Supplementary blinds, which block solar gain while allowing a low level of daylight to permeate the building, are fixed beneath the roof-lights.

For Loren Butt, determining the environmental strategy was partly a matter of rejecting conventional curatorial preferences – that is to say, for mechanical cooling and low light levels. In fact, the low-energy solution was to prove critical in terms of the building's future maintenance and running costs, which fell to the university – and perhaps its very survival as an institution. In the wake of the financial cutbacks that universities had to confront during the early 1980s, UEA calculated that it could not have afforded to run the building, had it been reliant on heavily energy-consuming air-conditioning systems.

A further fundamental element in the display strategy was the lighting and for advice Foster turned to Claude Engle, the American lighting designer, whose recent projects had included the East Wing of the National Gallery in Washington DC (opened in 1978). Engle, who was to become a collaborator on many future Foster projects, seconded a young designer, George Sexton, to work on the Sainsbury Centre. (Sexton would subsequently launch his own international practice on the strength of that collaboration.) The artificial lighting in the building was carefully coordinated with the natural lighting strategy, with spotlights used to pick out and dramatise objects in the collection.

The detailed design of the other spaces in the building had also to be considered. In the light of disquiet from some academic staff at the idea of teaching spaces being located alongside a public museum, the design of the studies and other spaces became the subject of intensive research. Full-size

Above: The cladding panels are removable by merely unfastening six bolts. Any part of the roof or walls can be changed from solid to glass or vice versa. The operation requires only two men and can be completed in as little as five minutes per panel.

Below: In 1988, after deterioration was found in the cladding panels – caused by a chemical reaction between the supposedly inert foam insulation and the aluminium skin – the Sainsbury Centre's cladding was replaced. Advances in pressing technology meant that the new panels could be flat. The new smooth white surface has lent the building a sleek quality, which is animated by the transition from solid to glazed sections.

Overleaf: At the building's open ends the glass wall is drawn back and the truss structure revealed; cross-bracing connects the two end trusses to give stability to the whole structure.

mock-ups of office and workshop spaces were constructed and members of the Foster team worked in them to assess how well they would suit their intended users. Significantly, when the Centre opened and staff and students were installed in their new accommodation, very few complaints were heard. The academics seemed to warm to their elevated common room and the restaurant at the western end of the building soon proved popular with the entire university community.

In his 1975 novel, *The History Man*, Malcolm Bradbury, a distinguished member of the UEA faculty, anticipated the attractions of 'the University's shining and metallic centre for the visual arts'. From the very beginning, the impact of the Sainsbury Centre on the life of the university and of Norwich more widely was notable. Under the leadership of the Centre's first director, Alan Borg, an inspired programme of temporary exhibitions added to the attractions of the permanent collection.

The first of these temporary exhibitions, which opened in November 1978, was devoted to the work of Charles and Ray Eames. In the absence of a curator at the time, Foster himself was instrumental in bringing the exhibition to UEA and designed the installation. It seems a highly appropriate choice, given the Eames' 'kit of parts' approach to the design of furniture and buildings, and the degree to which they saw the two disciplines as a unity.

The critical reaction to the Sainsbury Centre on its opening was generally enthusiastic. For Peter Cook, writing in *The Architectural Review*, the building was less radical than Willis Faber but had 'that special Foster quality that is so rare – even uncharacteristic in English architecture – which is strength of will.' Philip Johnson declared that 'There isn't anyone in America who could do something as good as the Sainsbury Centre. England has at once become the leader in the engineering and technology game.' Sutherland Lyall wrote memorably of 'the almost silent clatter of thousands of small plastic-coated parts every time a cloud goes by …'

However, there were naturally dissenting voices. Doug Clelland, writing in *Architectural Design*, saw the Centre as an example of 'fetishist expressionism … it is no more or no less interesting than a can of Campbell's – no – Sainsbury's soup.' Leon Krier, then a young AA radical, warmed to the 'elegance and dignity of Foster's Sainsbury shed', in contrast to the 'industrial crudeness and brutality' of Lasdun's UEA campus, but found it inappropriate as a container for art: 'Foster is forcing us to eat soup with a fork …' Robin Middleton

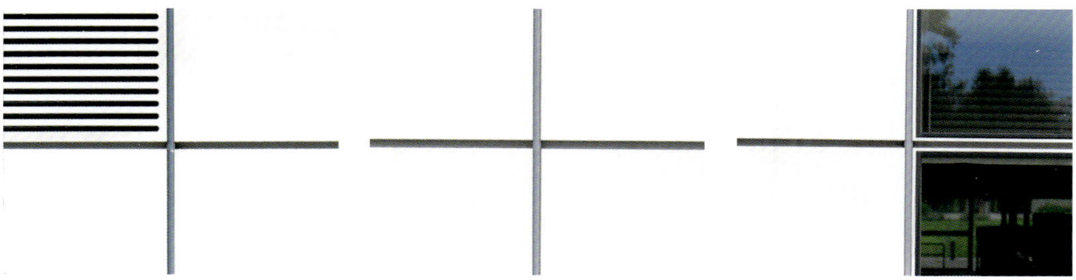

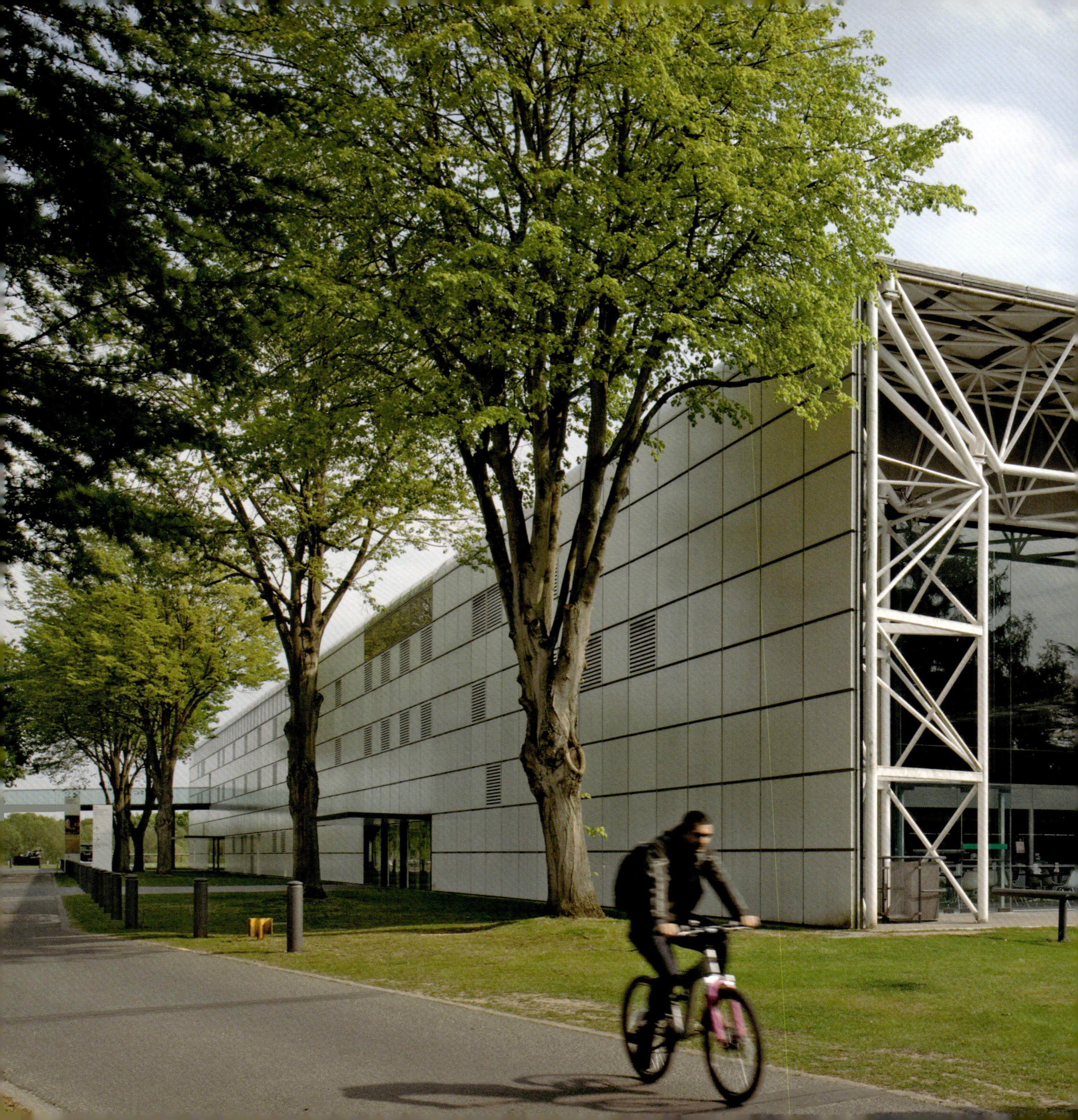

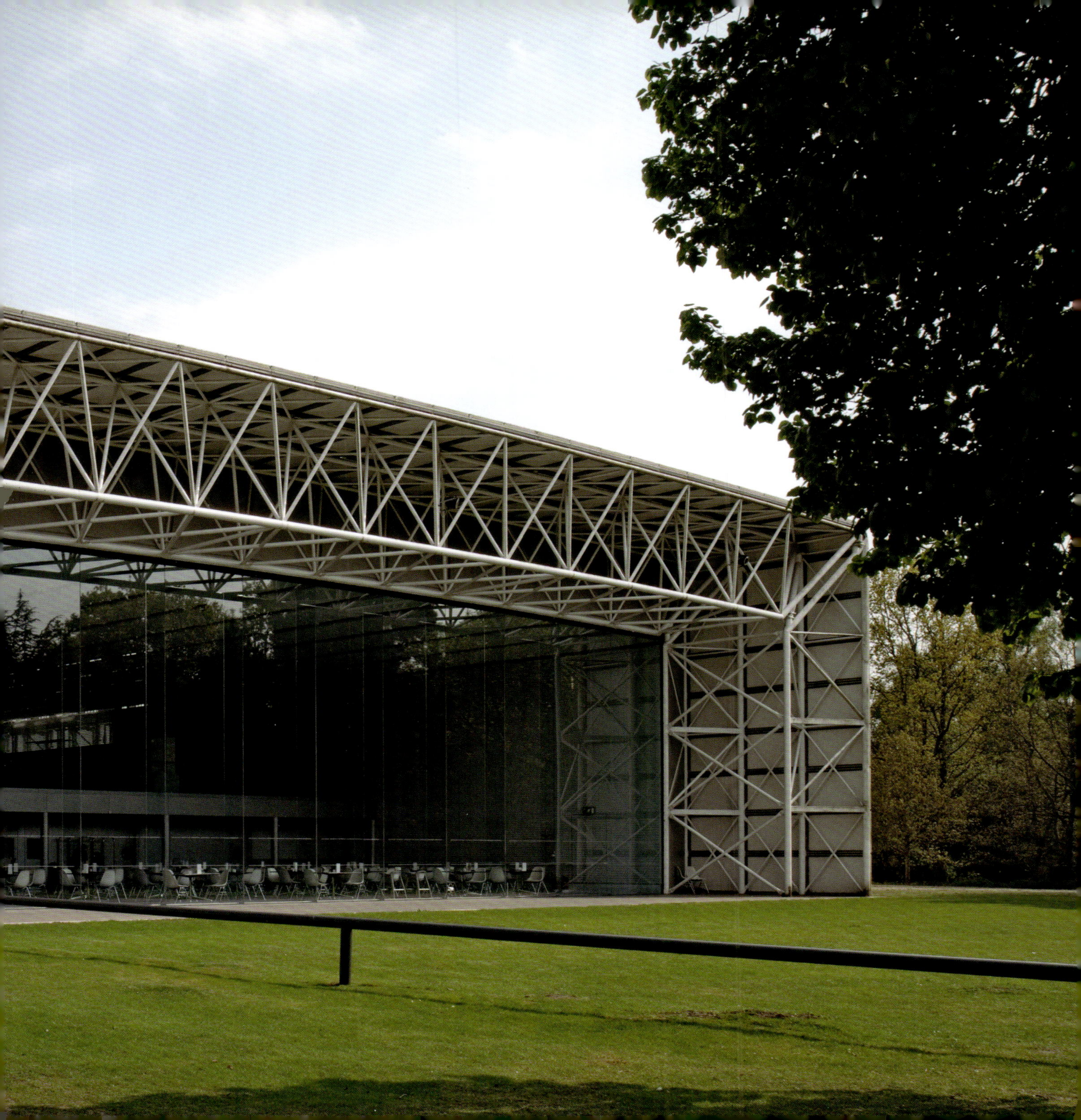

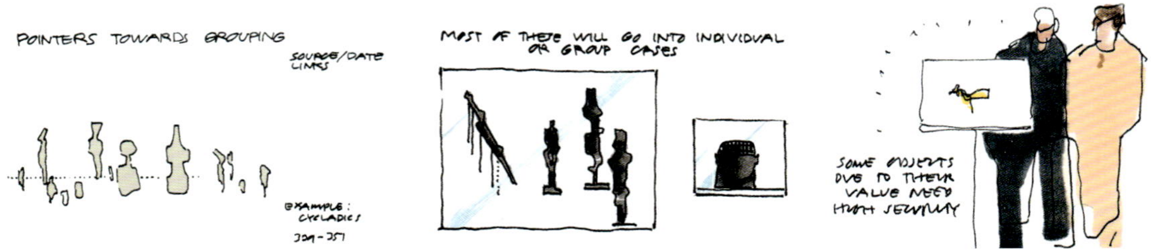

felt that 'richness and complexity have been sacrificed to a simplistic image'. The building had certainly provoked debate, much of it premonitory of the bitter style wars of the 1980s, the decade that saw Foster himself firmly established as a leading force on the global architecture scene.

The Sainsbury Centre, remarkably innovative as it was, almost inevitably encountered teething troubles. One affected the 70-metre long bridge, highly minimal in form, which had been designed to connect the building to Lasdun's upper-level walkway system. Fabricated of steel and glass, it terminated in a spiral stair with steel treads and risers cantilevered from a central steel column. Tony Hunt recalls a visit to the building, shortly before its opening, and seeing two colleagues standing on the bridge conversing. To his alarm, the bridge seemed to be swaying gently. Hunt re-examined his calculations and decided that the structure needed to be stiffened – but how could it be done? The flexibility of the building came into play at this point. It was a simple matter to remove some of the roof cladding panels. A crane was brought in and steel rods were dropped in and welded to the column.

This story brings to mind one of Foster's favourite analogies, in which he compares the building with a modern aircraft – while the airframe may be designed to fly thousands of hours, the engines and avionics will be replaced many times during its lifetime. The Sainsbury Centre was consciously designed to allow the 'short-life' items to be replaced with ease. When problems were detected with the cladding system, this approach would prove to be prescient.

Ironically, the most untried element of the cladding would prove to be the most durable. The lattice of neoprene (26 tonnes of it) – never before used on such a scale in a building project – which seals the panels and channels rainwater run-off, is still in perfect condition. It was the panels themselves that began to fail very soon after their installation. Within a month of the building's opening, it was noticed that some of the aluminium panels were exhibiting 'pitting' at their exposed corners. At first it was thought that some sort of reinforcement – 'suitcase corners' – could be applied where the aluminium was thinnest to remedy the problem. However, in due course the problem was to prove so fundamental that progressive replacement of some of the cladding had to be carried out.

The original cladding consisted of glazed or solid panels, each measuring 1.8 x 1.2 metres. The solid panels were of sandwich construction, with a thin skin of anodised superplastic aluminium bonded to a 75mm thick layer of insulating phenolic foam. The source of

Above: Birkin Haward analysed the Sainsbury collection and explored techniques for its display in a sequence of freehand drawings.

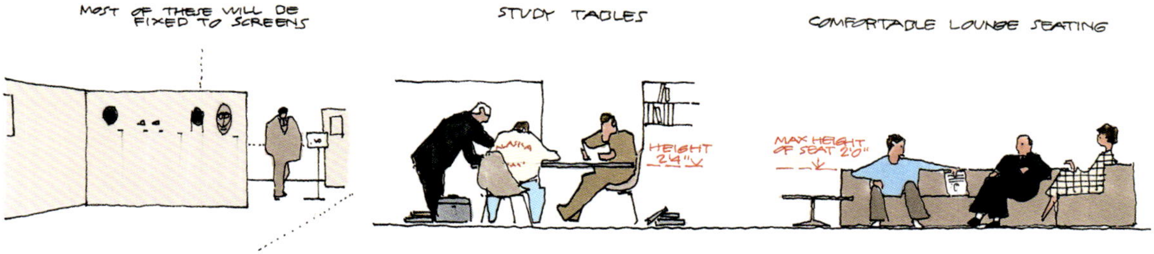

the 'pitting' problem, not initially identified, was a corrosive interaction between the aluminium and the phenolic foam. The foam had been guaranteed to be inert but in fact, because during manufacture it had not been allowed to cure properly, it proved destructively acidic. Foster describes the effect as like a 'cancer'. The manufacturer of the panels accepted responsibility and some of the units were replaced, like for like, with work starting in autumn 1978. Foster was philosophical about the matter – 'One of the strengths of the building was the fact that you could easily unbolt and replace the panels, along with other components,' he says.

Within a decade it had become apparent that the replacement panels themselves were failing. The root cause of the problem had never been adequately addressed by the manufacturer. A radical solution to the problem followed, with funding provided by the Sainsbury family (the cladding contractor having gone out of business). The building's entire cladding was replaced, with new panels strikingly different from the originals.

For Foster it was an opportunity to turn the aircraft analogy into reality; to improve the ultraviolet filtering of the glazed panels and to upgrade the technical performance of the cladding overall. The ribbed

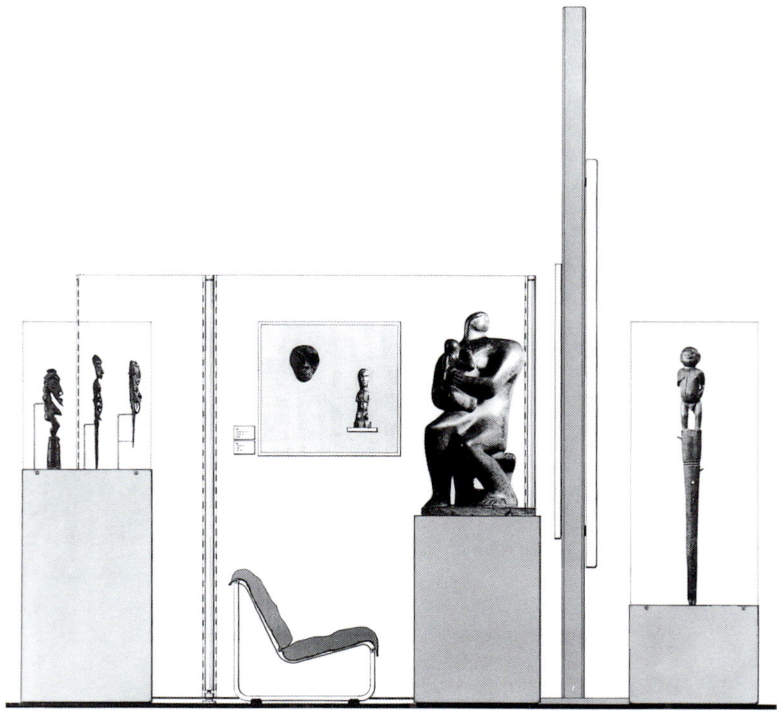

Above: The display system comprises freestanding panels, hinged screens, display cases, stand and plinths, creating a kit of parts with its own simple rules. Carefully arranged, the different elements allow the space to remain free, flowing and flexible.

Right: While display cases were standardised, each object in the collection required its own supporting armature to be specially made.

Far right: Sir Robert and Lady Sainsbury were involved at every stage of the design process and are seen here with Norman Foster reviewing the prototype display system.

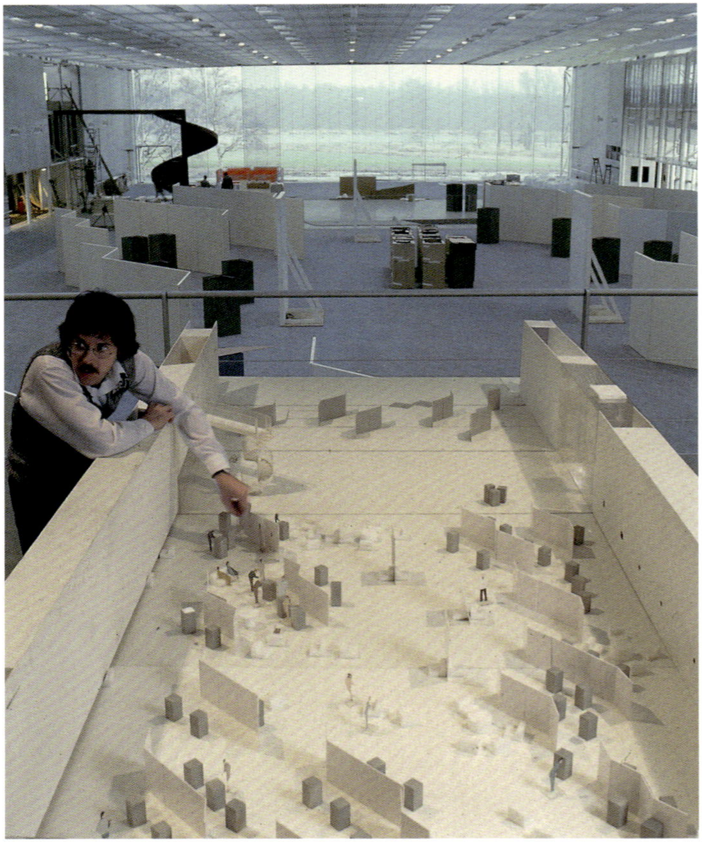

appearance of the original panels was not reproduced. Instead, panels of honeycomb aluminium, with rockwool insulation and a smooth white PVF2 finish, were installed. The brilliant white finish made sense environmentally (in terms of reducing solar gain – like cricketers' whites) but certainly changed the look of the building, giving it a sleek, glossy aesthetic. For one critic, the building's new livery was 'more Boeing 747 than Citroën van' – an observation with which Foster would happily concur.

From the very beginning – and as this episode reinforces – the Sainsburys were emphatically hands-on clients. Once the building had opened they had no intention of simply handing over their collection and going away. They maintained a close and active interest in the Sainsbury Centre after it opened, visiting it frequently and adding further works of art to the original, remarkable gift.

By the mid-1980s, the Sainsbury Centre's popularity and the intensive use made of the building, including exhibitions, conferences and other events, was beginning to place a strain on its facilities. Furthermore, a considerable part of the collection could not be shown in the main gallery but had to be kept in storage, where it was inaccessible to visitors. It was in 1986 that the idea of extending the building first

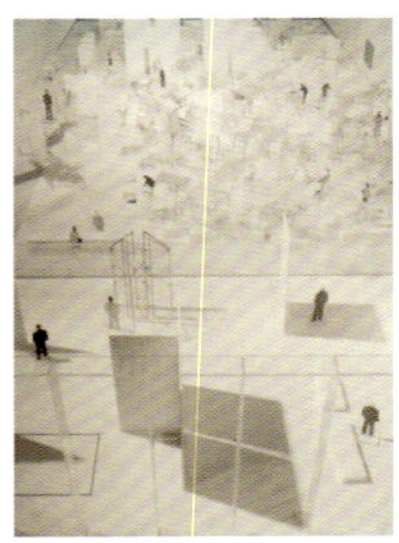

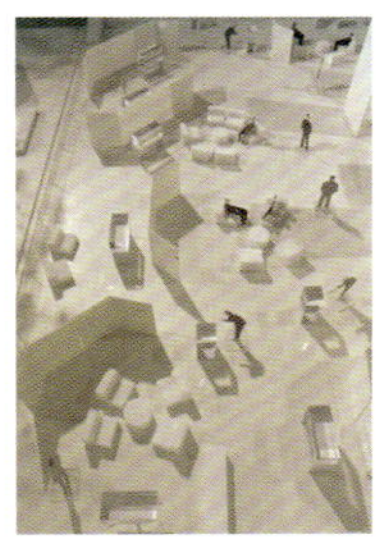

Above and right: A detailed scale model was prepared as an aid to setting out the display system. A key objective was to encourage a rich mix between people and art objects; seating was an important ingredient, helping to create places to relax, sit and read or contemplate the works on display.

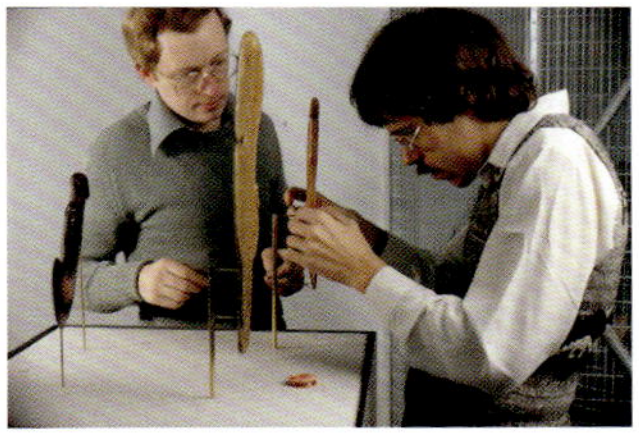

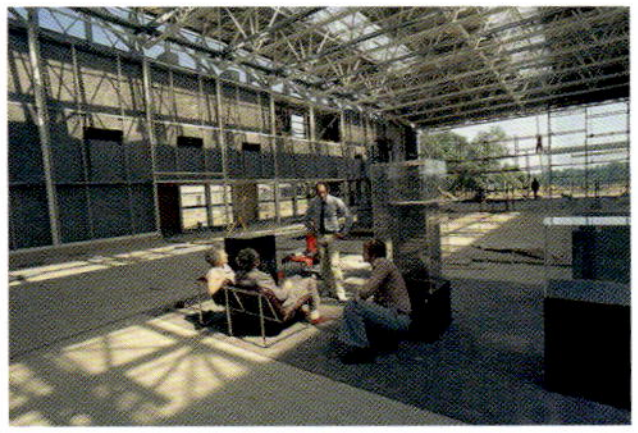

came under active discussion. Foster had always foreseen the possibility of an extension, which would naturally take place on land to the east of the Centre, towards the lake. Given the character of the building, the natural way to extend it was simply to extrude the original envelope and Foster produced some sketches showing how this might be done. The Sainsburys were, however, unhappy with the idea – the Centre was, for Sir Robert, nothing less than 'the greatest work in our collection'.

Nor was Foster himself entirely convinced that it was the right way forward – 'we don't do the obvious', he commented, 'we are always open-minded, ready to discard our preconceptions.' One possible solution was to create a new building on adjacent land, screened by trees, and link it to the Centre by means of an underground passage. But this idea was quickly ruled out on grounds of security, convenience, cost – and architectural logic. So the idea emerged of an addition which would form an extension to the existing basement level and take advantage of the fall in the landscape to the east.

The Sainsburys liked the idea: 'It seems to us to solve our problems in a most satisfactory way with a more straightforward design and probably less difficulty with planning permissions,' Robert Sainsbury wrote to Foster in November 1987. (Sainsbury subsequently raised concerns about possible water ingress into the building, which were allayed by Tony Hunt, as structural engineer for the project.)

What became the Crescent Wing was developed by the Foster team from a demanding brief. The Sainsburys had visited the study centre at the Metropolitan Museum of Art in New York, where pictures not on display in the galleries are kept secure but accessible in a system of sliding glass cases.

Such a facility, they felt, could be created at UEA. The Centre's curators had also identified a need for more workshop and laboratory space, while the existing administrative offices were desperately cramped and the number of staff working in them had increased. The detailed schedule of accommodation that subsequently emerged envisaged a building of 2,300 square metres, bringing the total area to some 6,000 square metres.

The Crescent Wing would be a partly day-lit, partly subterranean structure. This division actually fitted well with the brief. Offices needed good natural light, for example, while photographic darkrooms needed to be capable of total black-out. Providing the requisite amount of day-lit office space was a particular conundrum, since the end elevation of the Centre

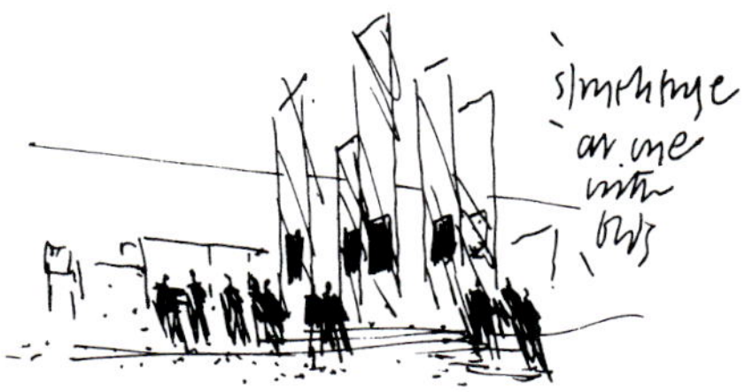

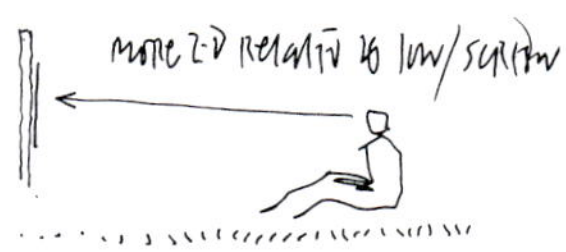

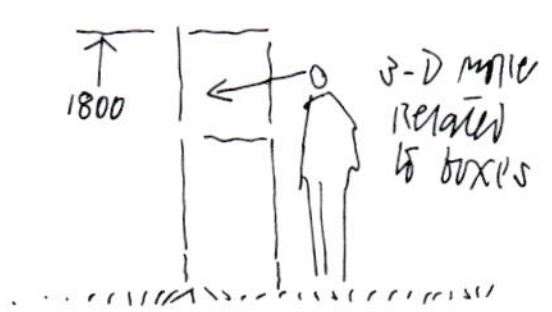

Left: Norman Foster's sketches explore options for the display of two- and three-dimensional works and how they might be viewed.

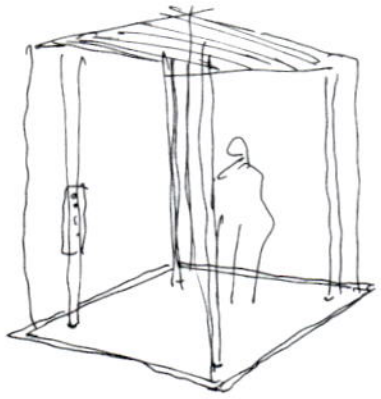

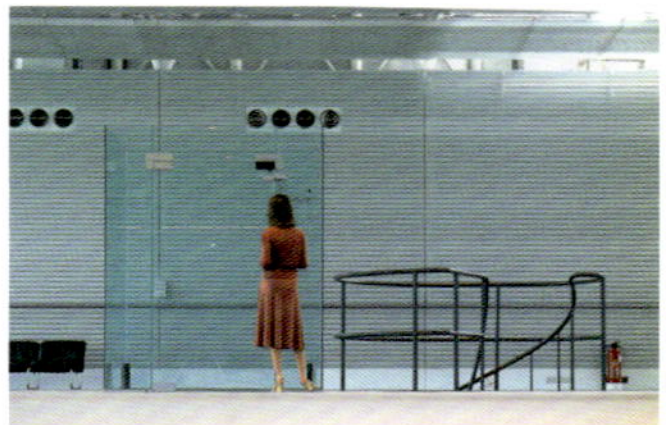

Far left, left: Toughened glass enclosures to lift-shaft and lift-cars minimise their visual impact. Norman Foster's sketch shows glass walls cladding a minimal steel frame.

is relatively narrow. If the building's footprint was simply extruded it limited the number of rooms that could benefit from light and views. In one of those adroit moves that have come to characterise his work, Foster came up with the idea of the curve or crescent – an innovation he describes as 'more radical than extending the original building; it was a response to real needs, a natural solution.'

It also offered a dynamic counterpoint to the existing shed. With its glassy form emerging from the landscape, it echoed – albeit on a far larger scale – the little Cockpit retreat at Feock in Cornwall that Foster had designed for the Brumwell family back in his Team 4 days. In retrospect, it is obvious that the Crescent Wing also looked forward as well as back, representing a move away from a generally rectilinear geometry towards a more organic architecture, which became apparent in the work of the Foster office in the 1990s.

At a stroke, the problem of how to incorporate an adequate area of day-lit offices was solved. Arranged along the sweep of the crescent, looking out across parkland to the lake, they are all square in plan, with only a slight canting of the walls to accommodate the curve. The planning of the other spaces was to prove more difficult. The challenge was to reconcile the rectilinear geometry derived from the original building and the curvilinear form of the new extension. 'We really struggled to resolve the plan successfully,' says Graham Phillips, the Foster partner who led the Crescent Wing team.

The lecture room, which was required to double as an occasional gallery, eventually became the pivot on which the difficulties of the plan were resolved. By making the space triangular the team was able to slot all the other accommodation into place, with the space for the reserve collection located to the east, where it abutted a ramp down to the lecture room.

In terms of connectivity, the relationship between the Crescent Wing and the original Sainsbury Centre remained somewhat ill-defined. If it was an extension to the latter, presumably it could be entered through the existing building? The Sainsburys took a different view – they were keen for it to have its own identity and a separate entrance.

That option was made all the more attractive by the university's reluctance to close the building to allow the extensive remodelling at basement level that would be required to create public access. This decision prompted a dramatic device: a long, glass-roofed ramp leading down to a new reception area with a fine view out.

Right: As completed in 1978, a reception desk combined information and sales areas with the gallery's central lighting and environmental control panel; a spiral stair led down to staff facilities in the undercroft.

Far right: The study reserve area was originally housed beneath the east mezzanine. Following the construction of the Crescent Wing, this space is now occupied by the Sainsbury Research Unit Library.

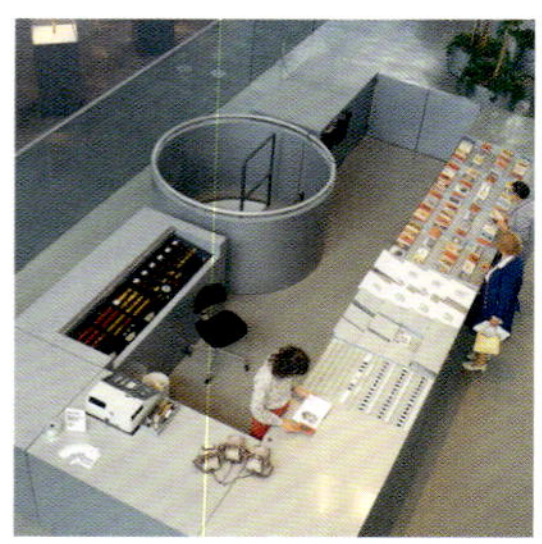

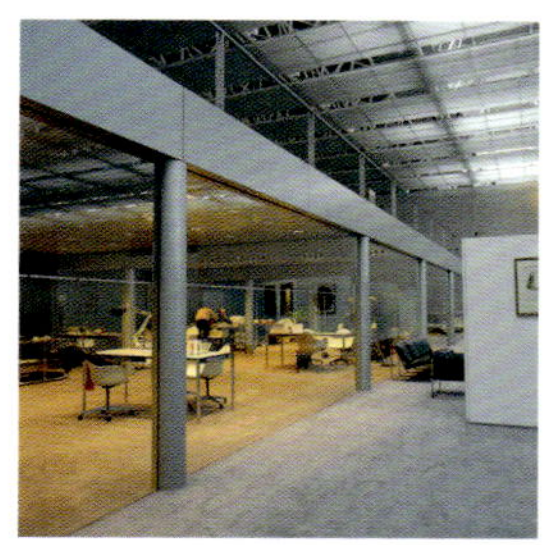

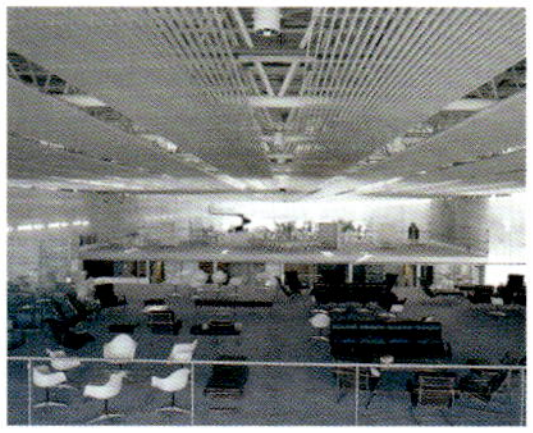

Left: A high-level view from the western end of the building in 1978. The senior common room and postgraduate desk area occupy the mezzanine in the foreground, overlooking the study/library area of the School of Fine Art beyond.

Until the recent alterations to the building, the reception area prefaced the private offices and functioned as the public entrance to the reserve collection and lecture room. Beyond this public area is a secure zone of stores, workshops and laboratories, tailored to the specific needs of curators, conservators and technicians, which connect seamlessly with the undercroft of the original building. These spaces are all generous in scale and well-finished and the work done in them is a vital part of the daily life of Centre. They are mechanically cooled and ventilated, with sophisticated extraction and filtration systems in the workshops and laboratories to cope with chemical fumes and dust. All these spaces are well insulated by the deep layer of earth on the roof, which greatly reduces their energy requirements.

The office spaces are naturally ventilated, with adjustable blinds to give users a degree of control over their working environment. The glazed elevation that lines the corridor in front of the offices was originally to consist of vertical glass panels, with a sloping bank of louvres to form a sun screen and to mould the elevation to the contours of the land. However, by using fritted glass – a material widely used by Foster to control natural light and baffle solar gain (in which the glass is screen-printed with a fine pattern of dots)

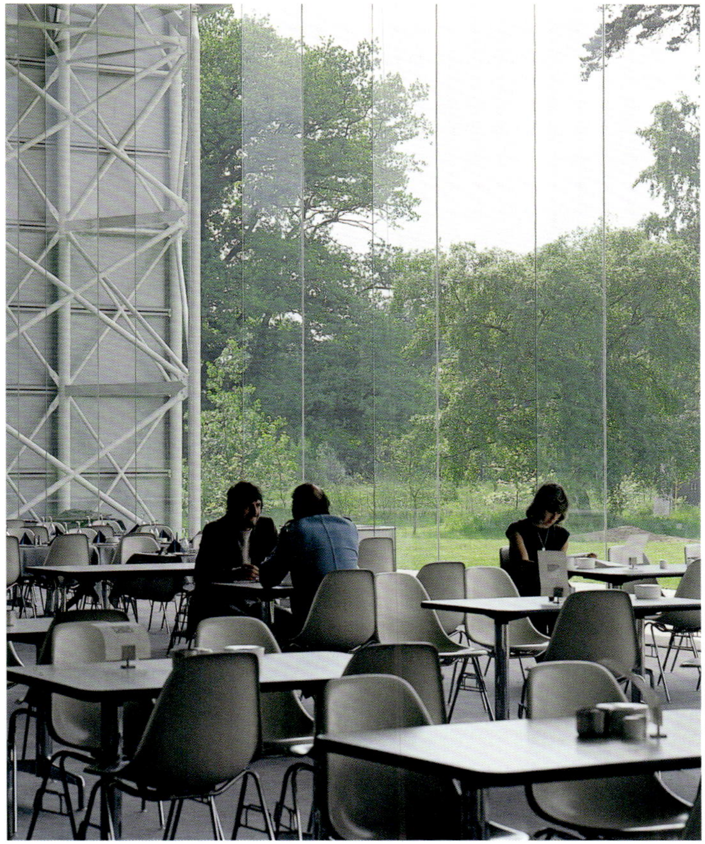

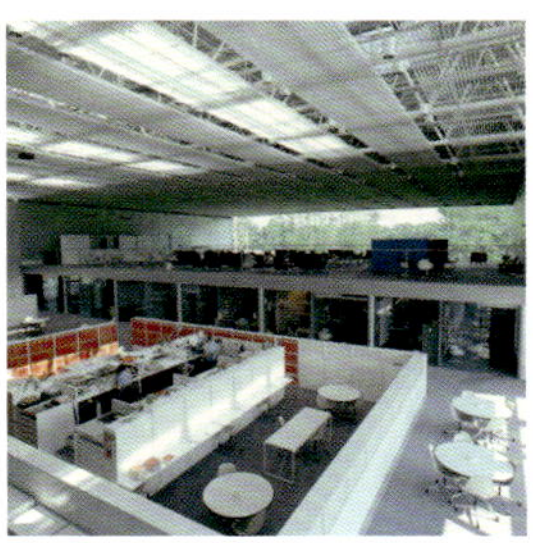

Above: The restaurant, photographed shortly after the building opened.

Left: The slide library in what was then the School of Fine Art, as completed in 1978. The cabinets were positioned to form a quiet study area.

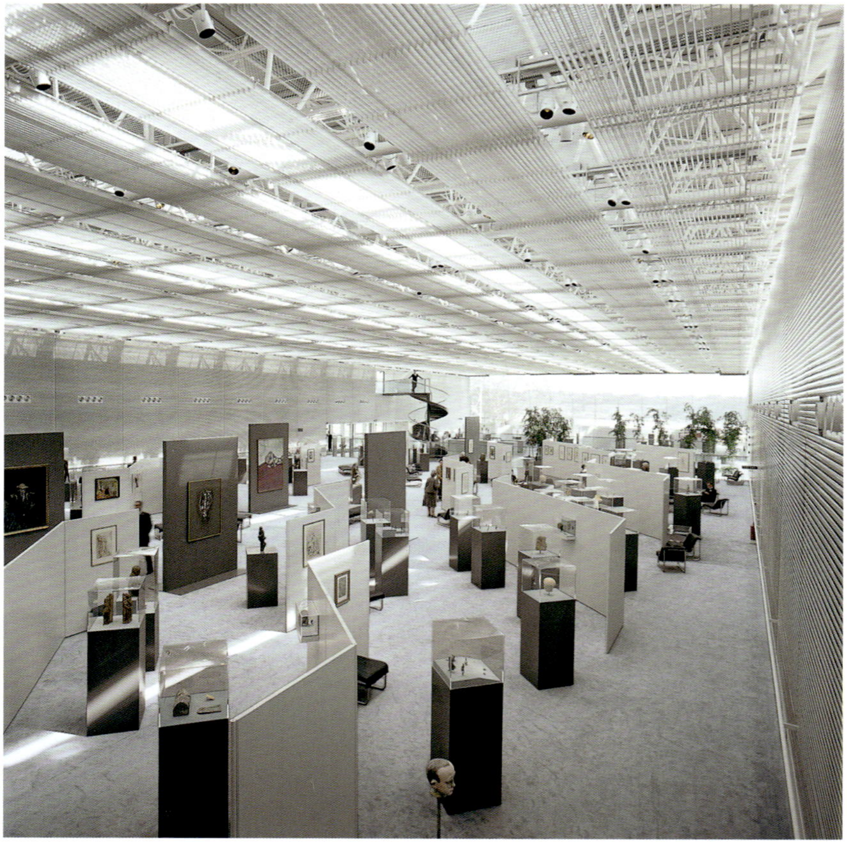

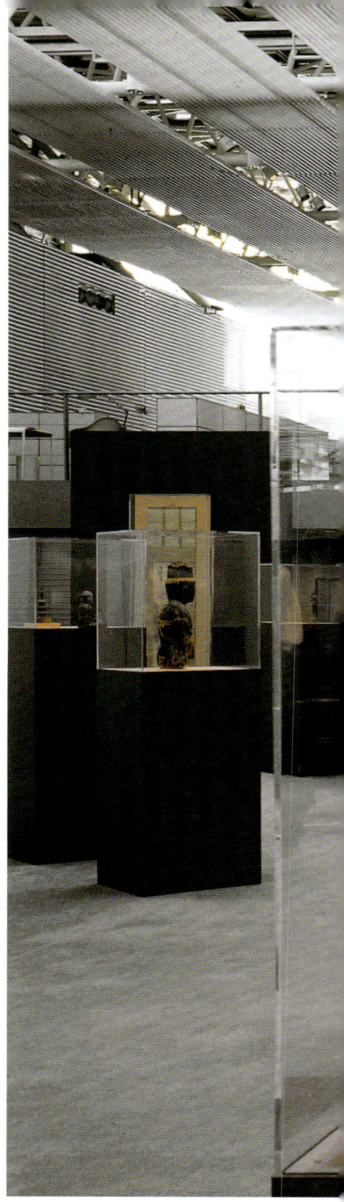

Above and right: The great enclosure of the Sainsbury Centre challenges the traditional division and social use of space in museums: here galleries and teaching spaces, students, academics and the public are brought together to create a dynamic unified space.

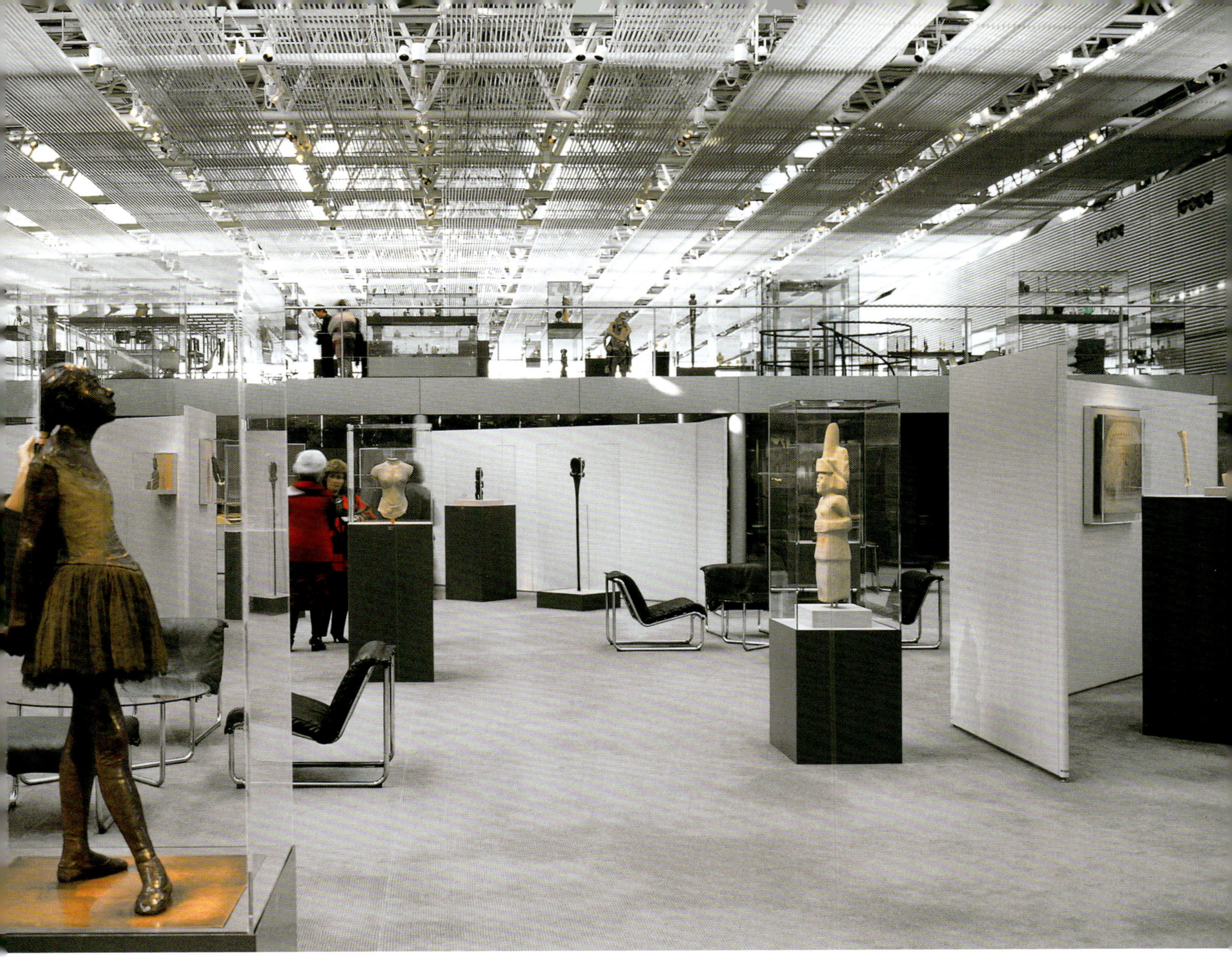

I'm not sure whether the original intention between Norman Foster and Bob Sainsbury – even if it wasn't articulated – was to make a total work of art. But that is what it has become.
Nichola Johnson, Director of the Sainsbury Centre for Visual Arts, 2009

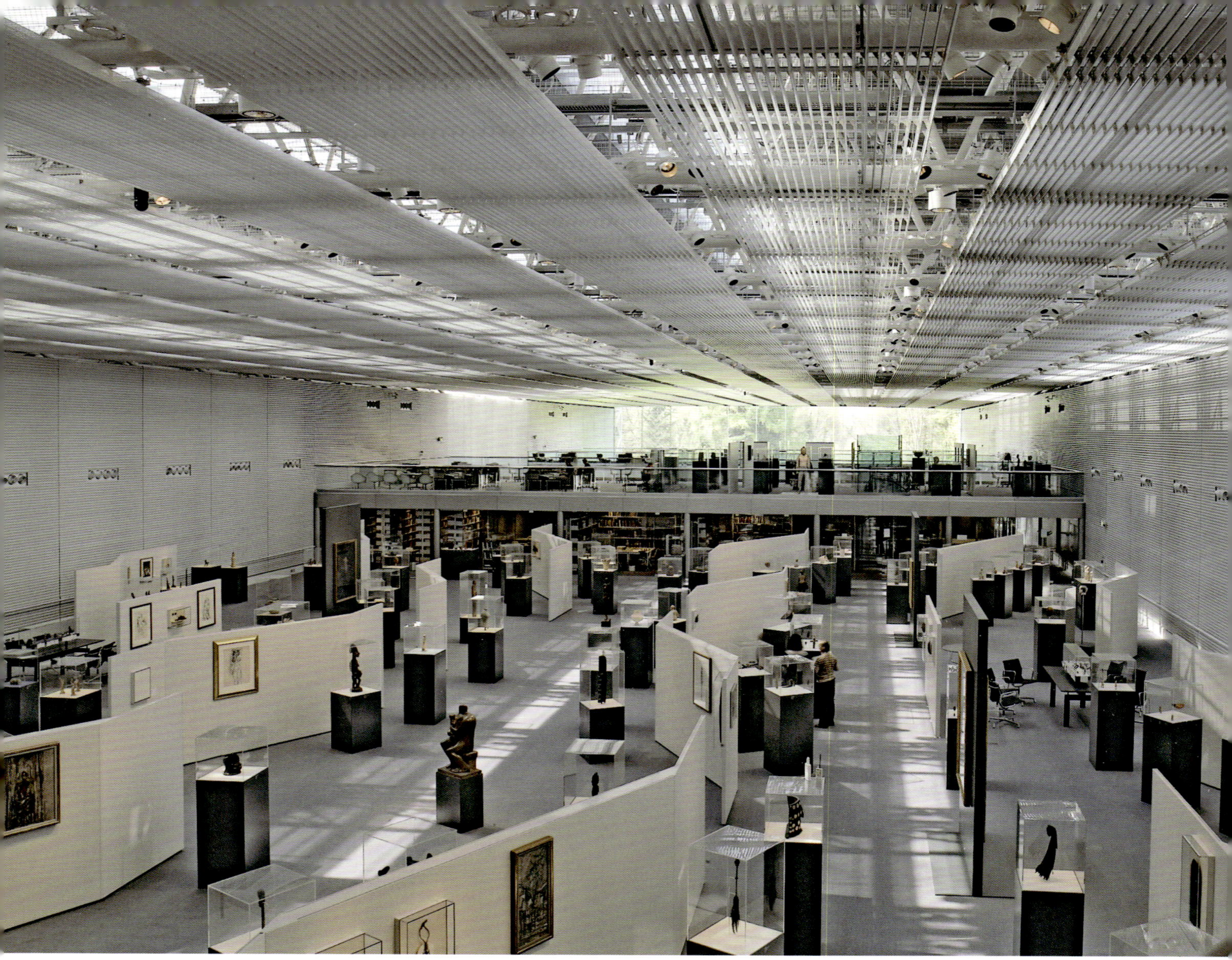

The openness of the building is wonderful – there's a sense of unfolding discovery about it, which makes it a very good vehicle for teaching. Veronica Sekules, Head of Education and Research, Sainsbury Centre for Visual Arts, 2009

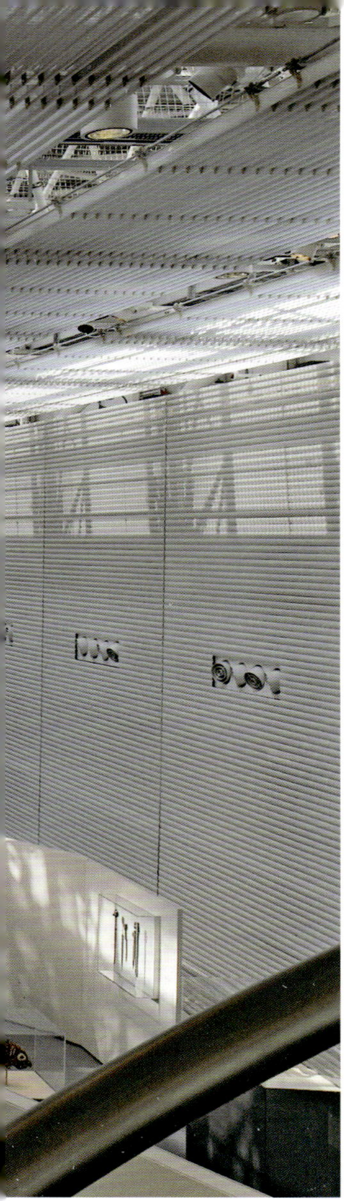

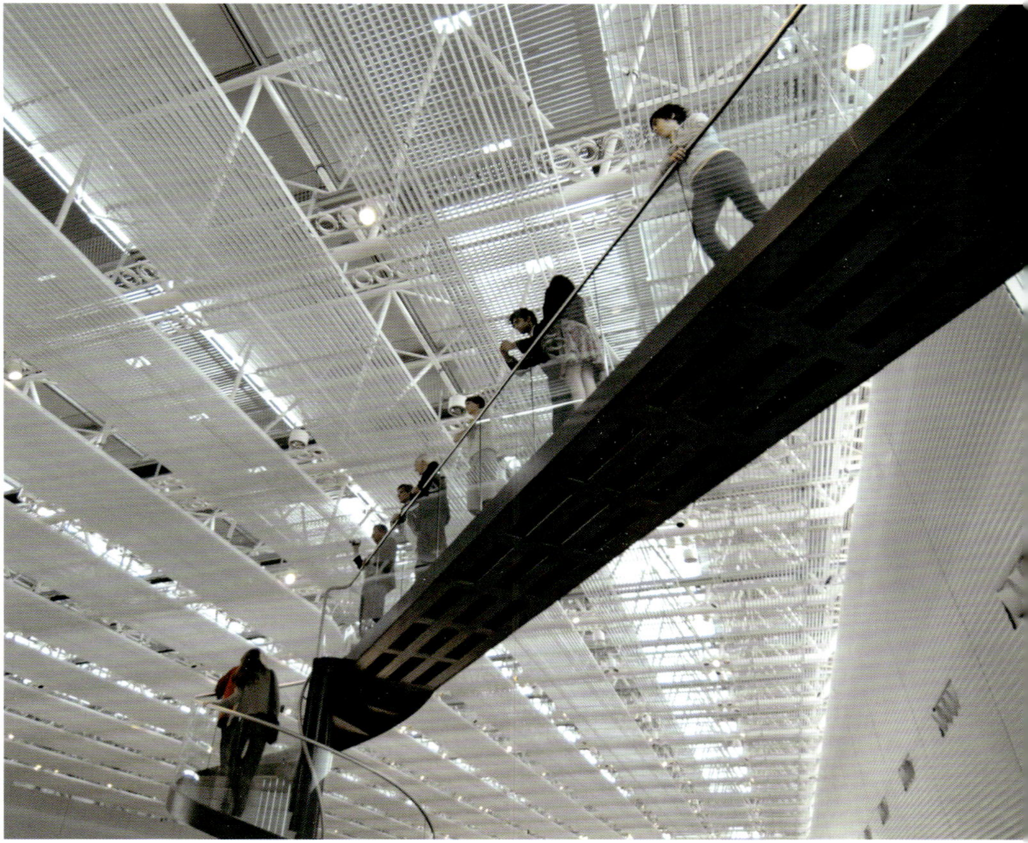

Above and right: Visitors entering the building from the elevated bridge link have a commanding view across the 'living area' gallery and the School of World Art Studies beyond.

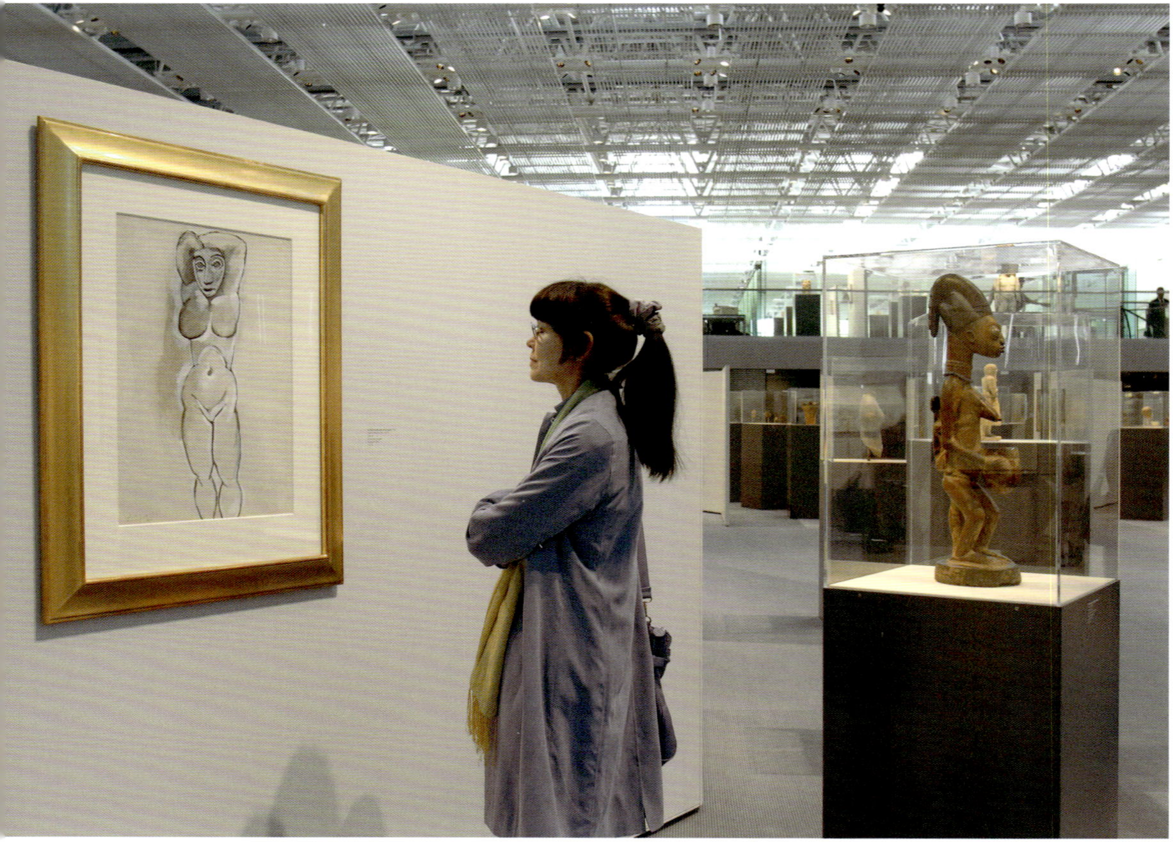

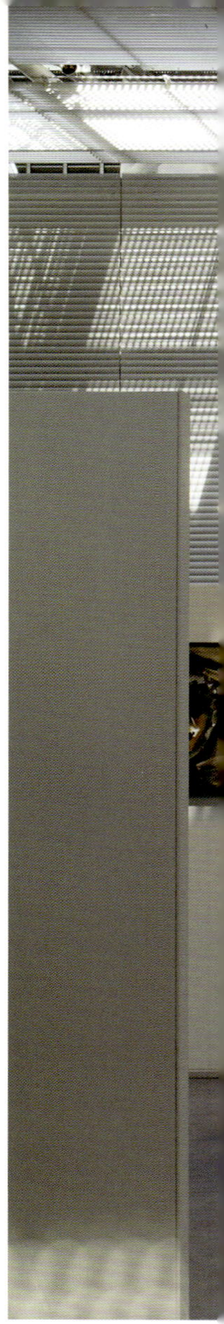

Above and right: In 2006 the Sainsbury Centre was completely overhauled and the permanent exhibition was rehung, though the essential spirit of the 'living area' and the evocation of a domestic setting are preserved.

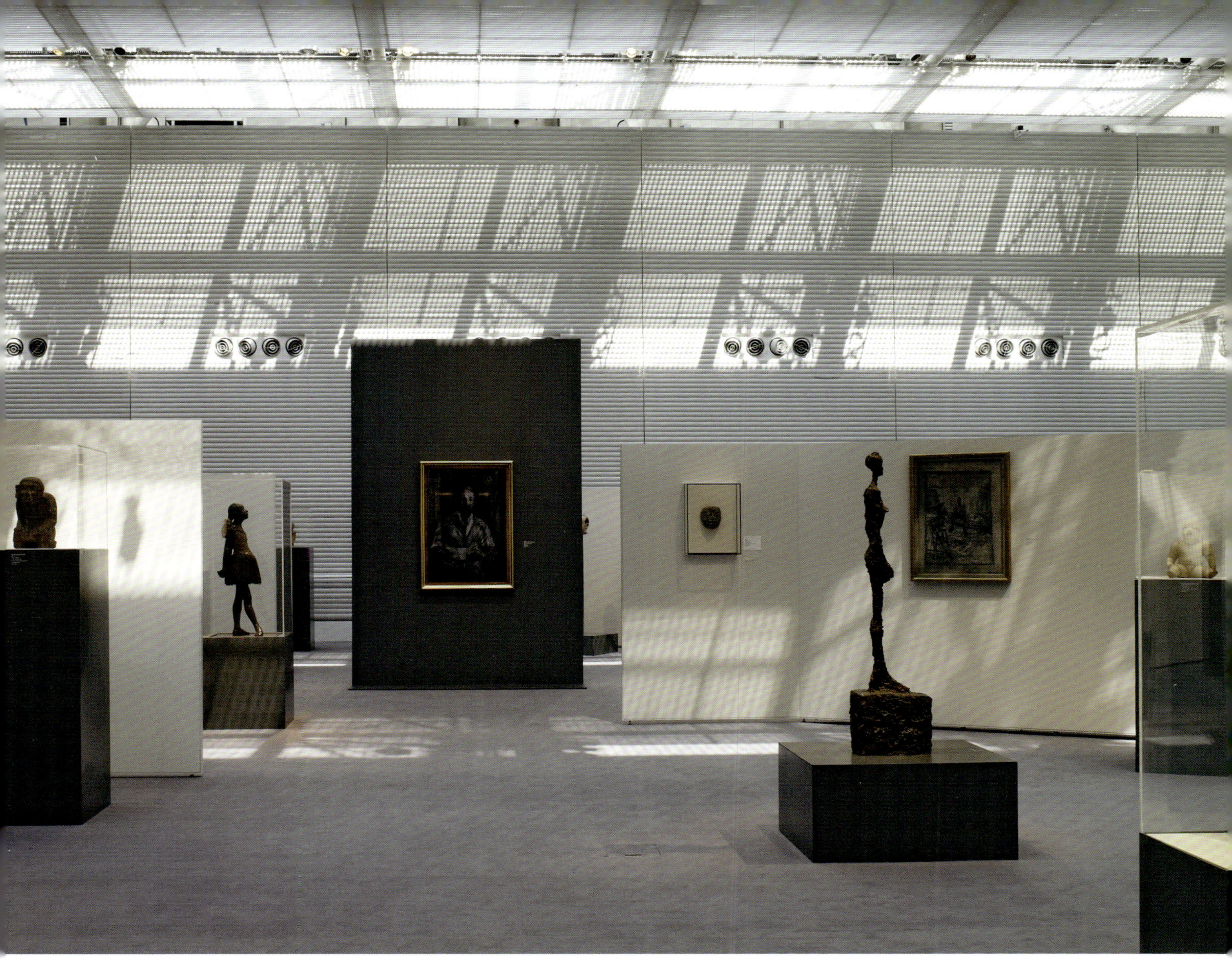

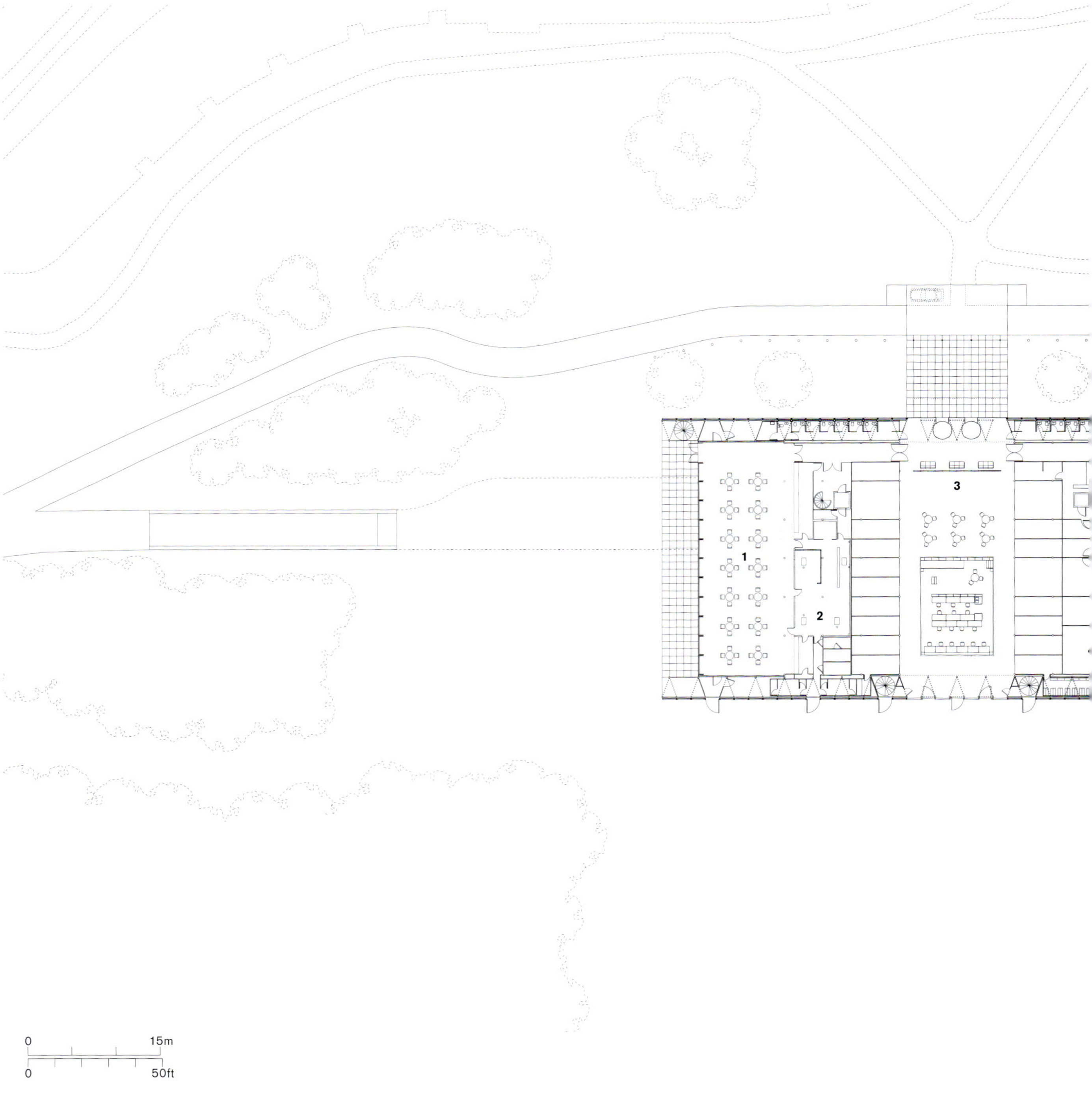
1
2
3
0
15m
0
50ft

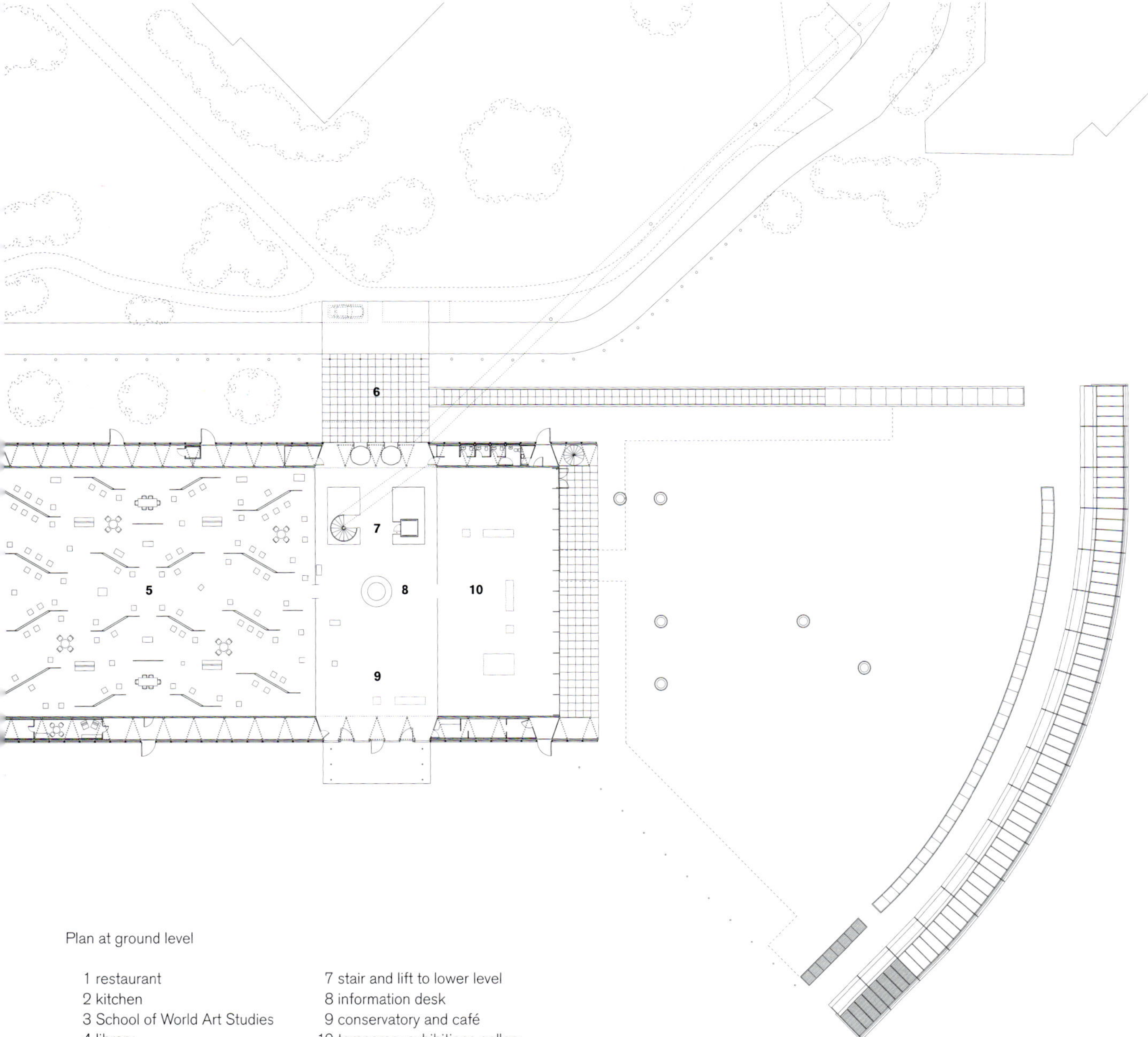

Plan at ground level

1 restaurant
2 kitchen
3 School of World Art Studies
4 library
5 'living area' gallery
6 main entrance
7 stair and lift to lower level
8 information desk
9 conservatory and café
10 temporary exhibitions gallery

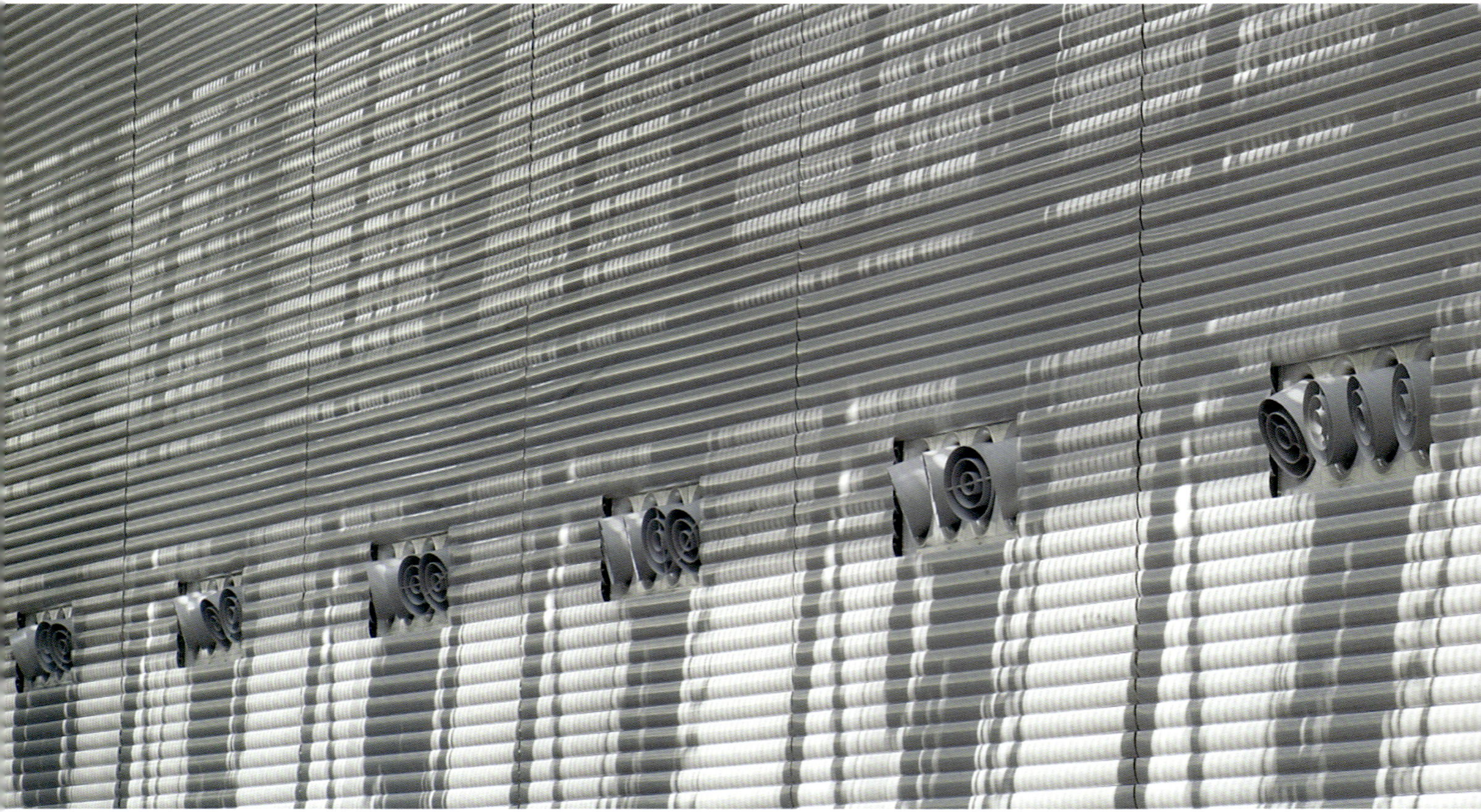

The constantly changing play
of light and shade across
and through the louvred
walls and soffit is one of
the Sainsbury Centre's most
remarkable characteristics.

The louvres under the windows are electronically controlled but you can override them. The technology itself is simple; there are no computers or anything like that. It is fairly down to earth, but it is still a very sensitive machine. Norman Foster, 2010

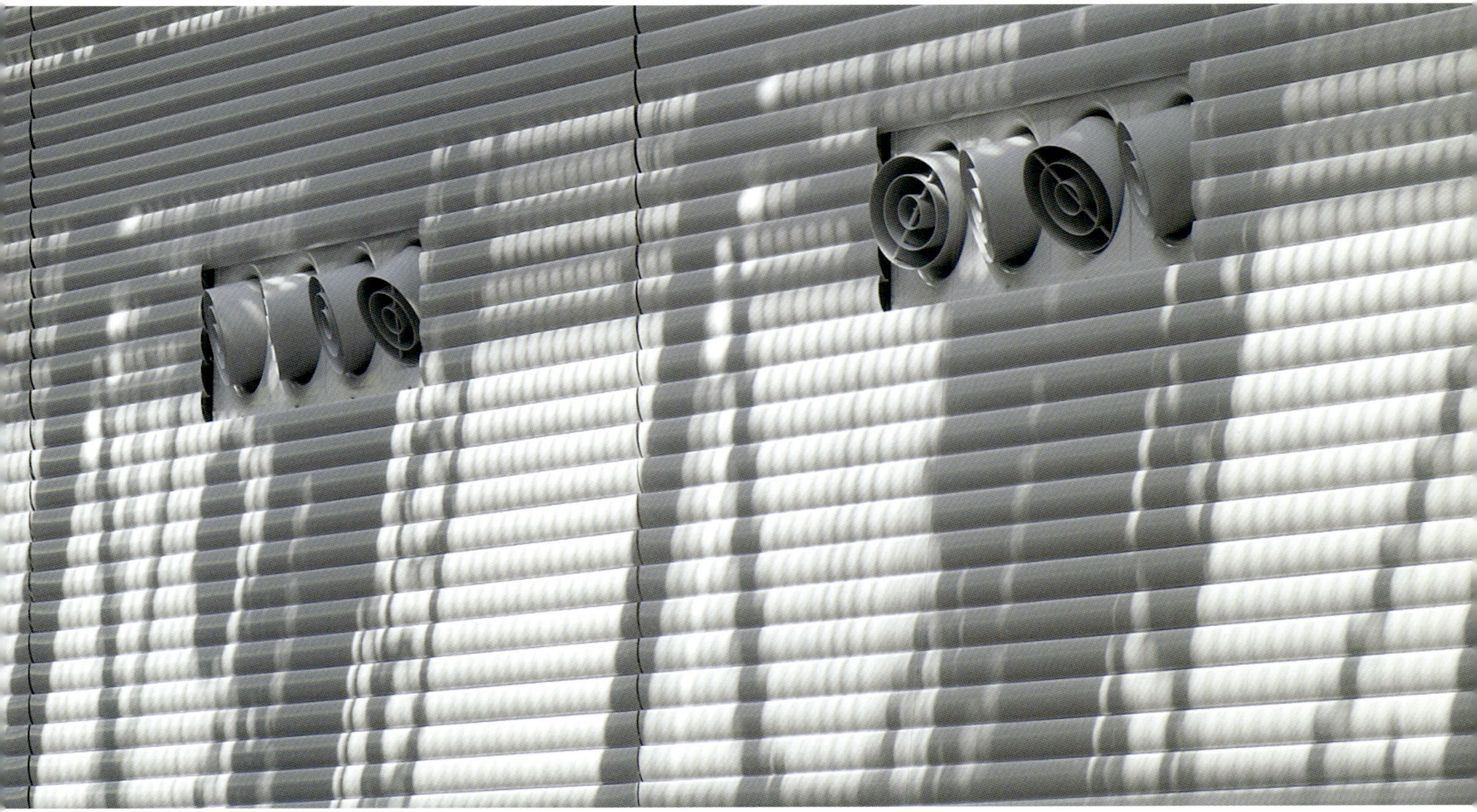

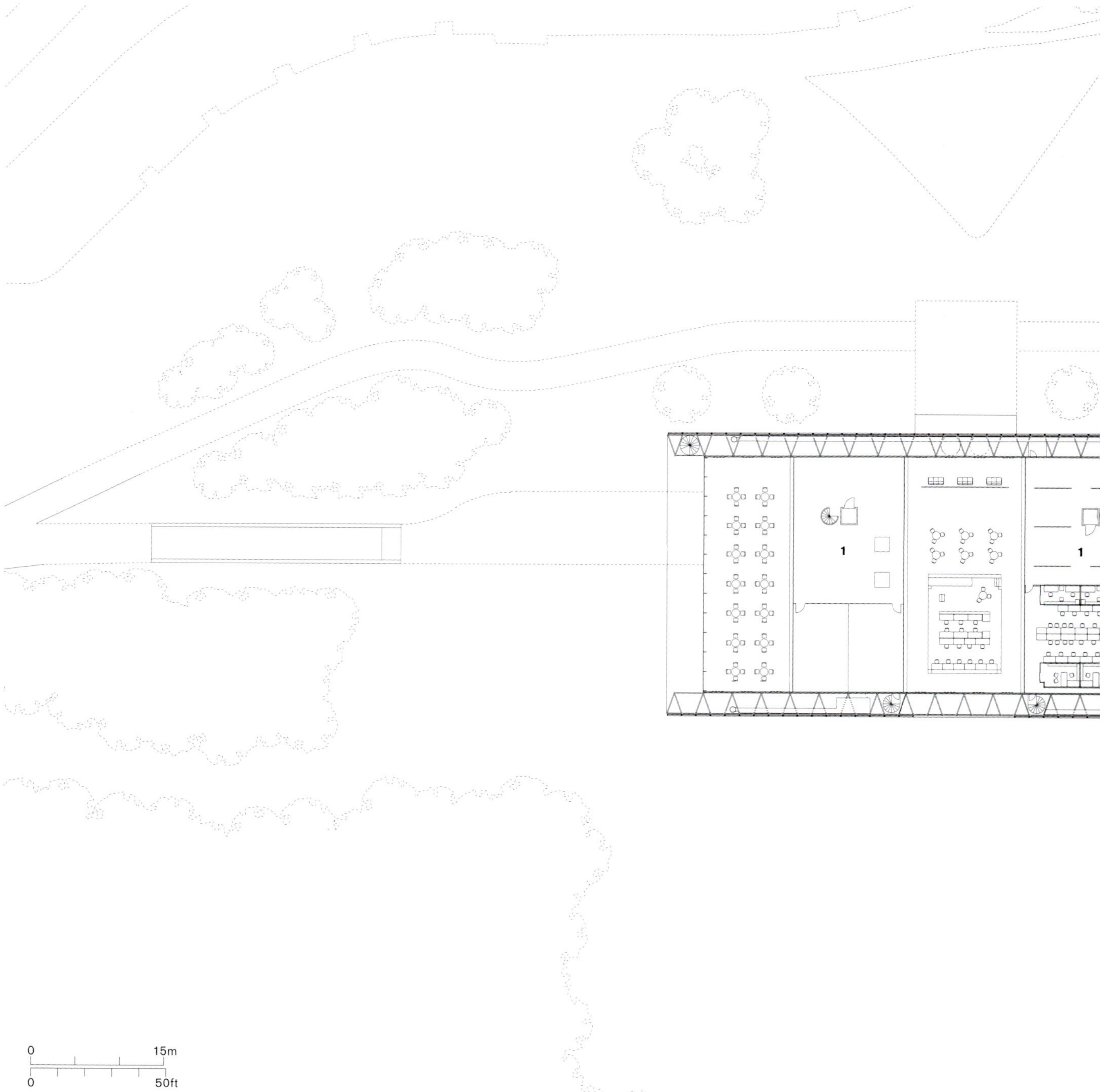
1
1
0
15m
0
50ft

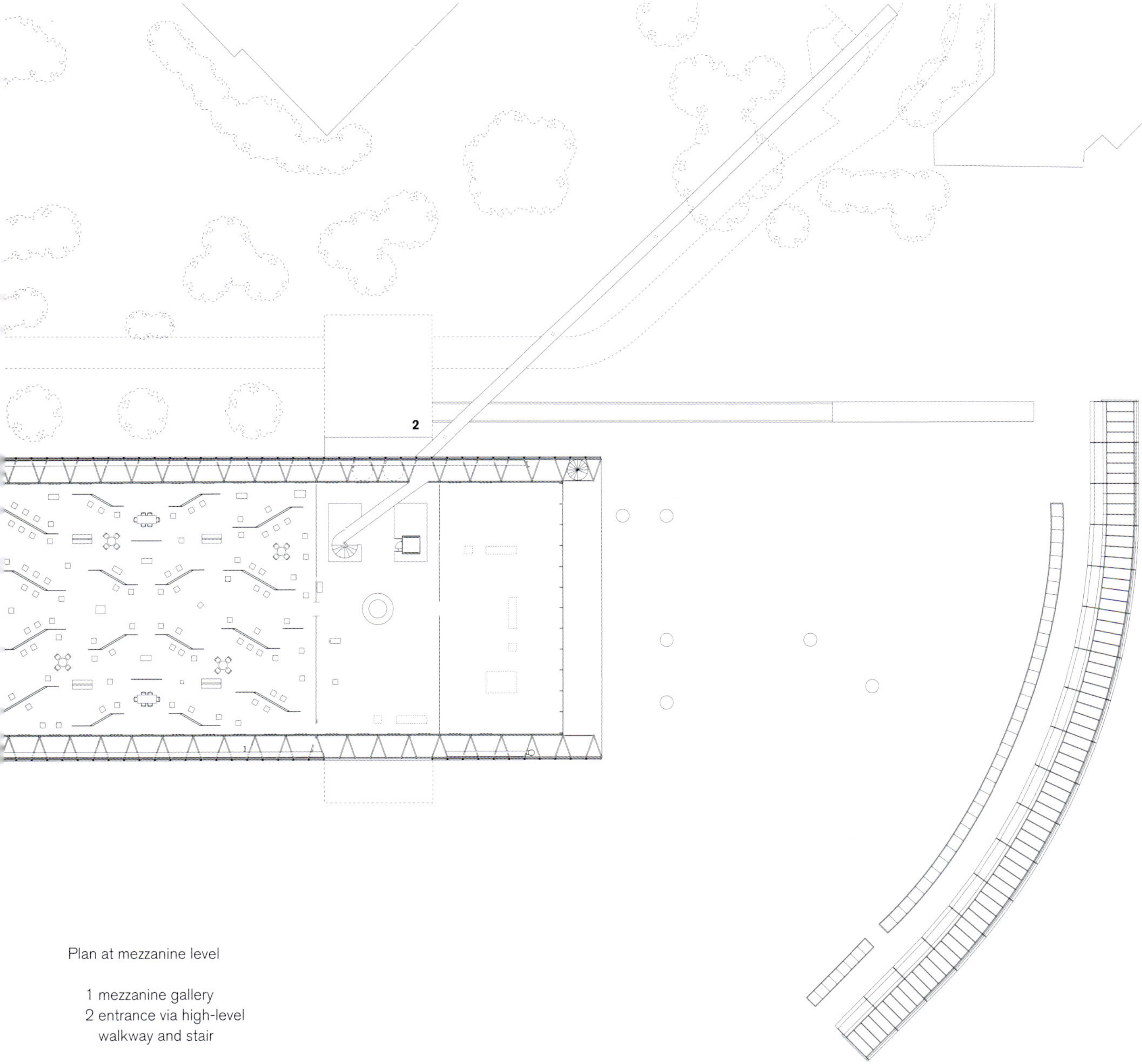

Plan at mezzanine level

1 mezzanine gallery
2 entrance via high-level walkway and stair

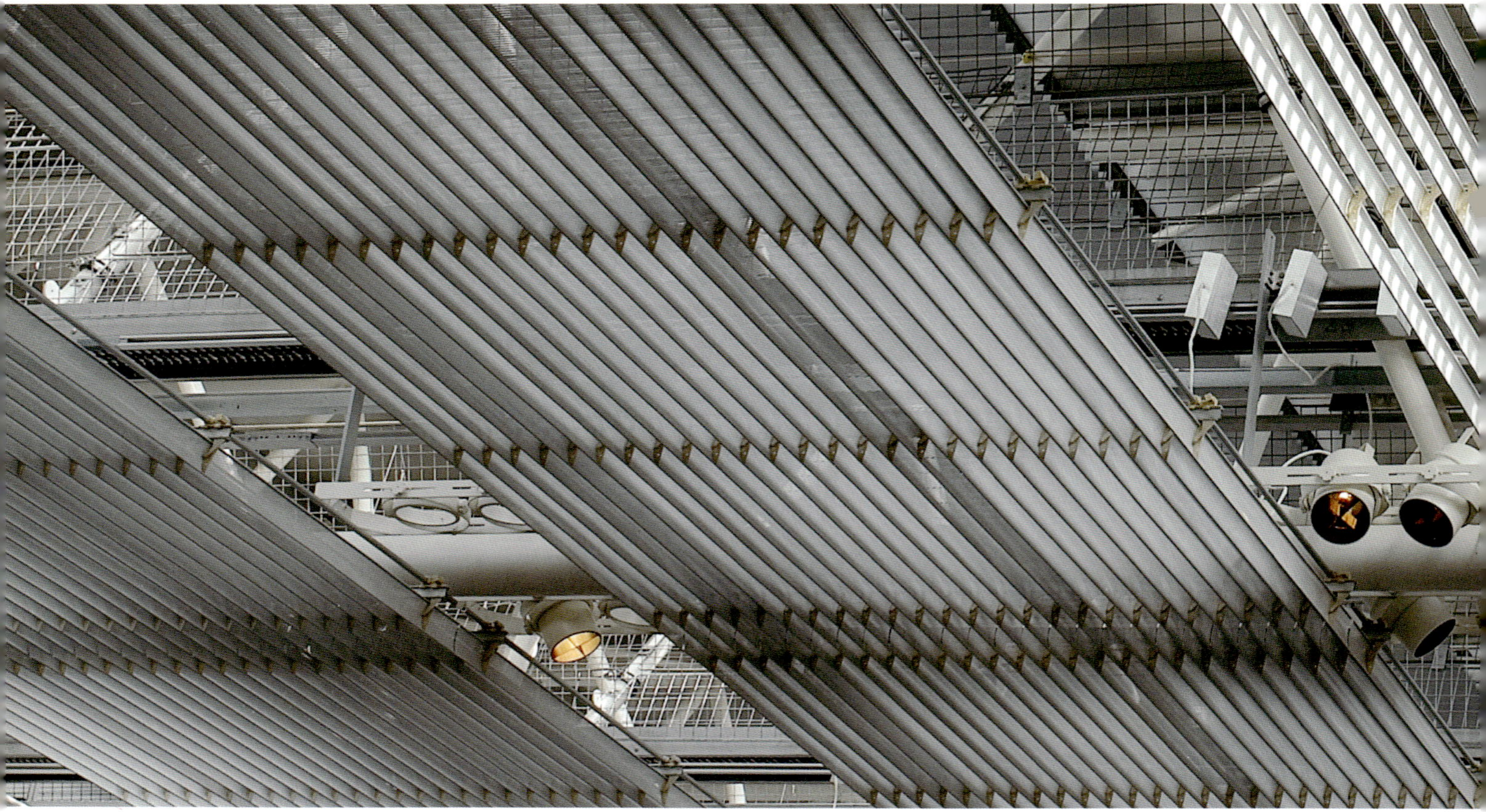

Artificial lighting is carefully coordinated with daylight admitted through the roof-lights. Ultra-violet light is filtered out by specially tinted glazing. Spotlights provide emphasis and create points of focus.

Motorized louvres buzz overhead to set up optical as well as acoustic vibrations. A delicate, dappled, even light spills over the space, equating all parts. Charles Jencks, *Current Architecture*, 1982

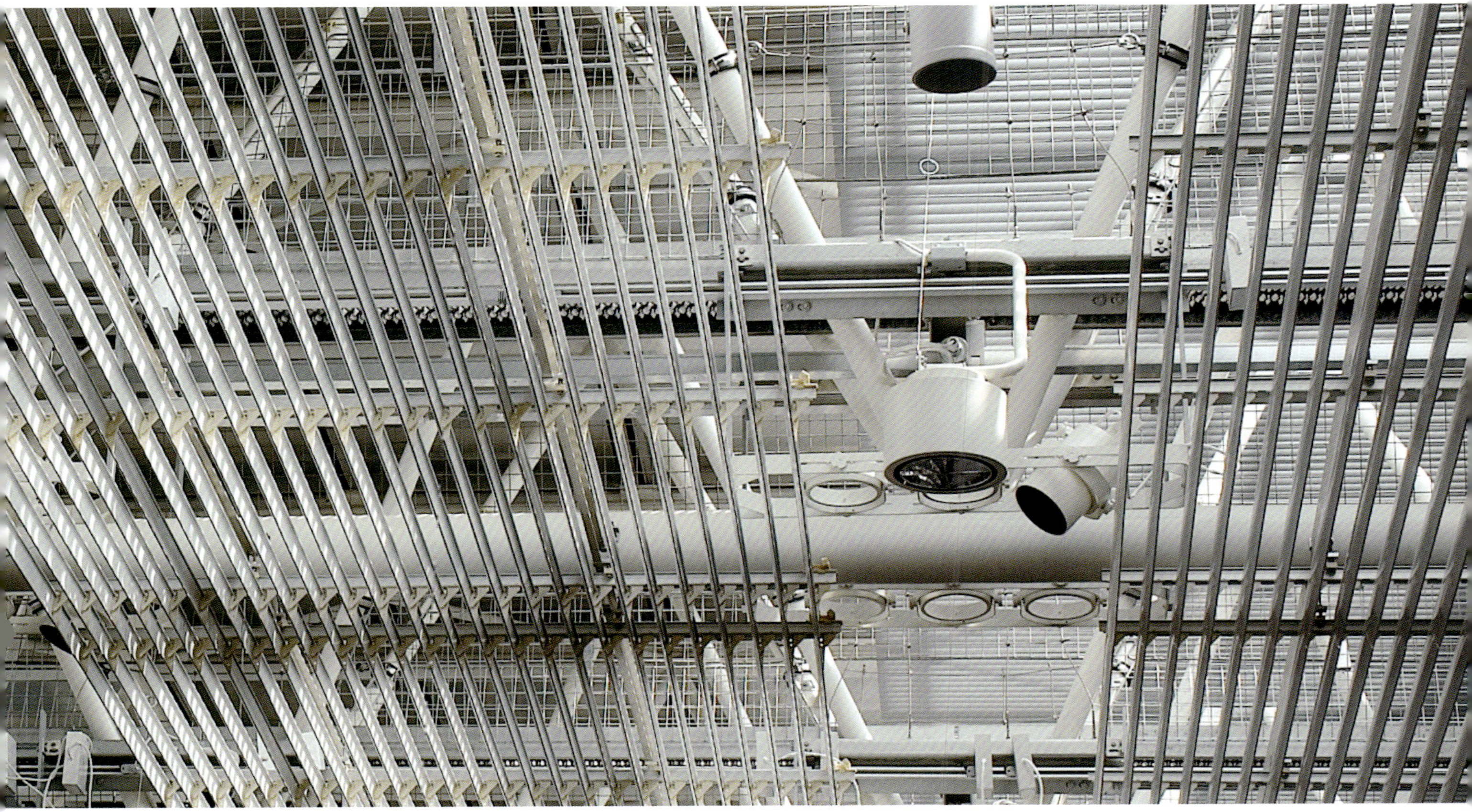

Plan at undercroft level

1 loading bay
2 shop
3 education centre
4 workshops
5 art handling and storage
6 conservation laboratory
7 seminar rooms
8 lower gallery
9 reserve collection
10 staff offices

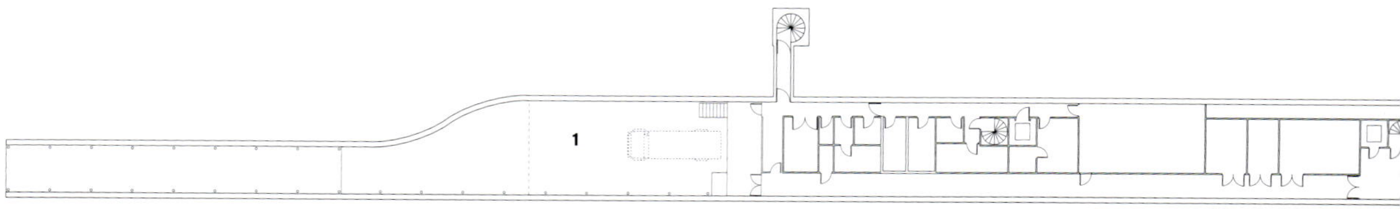

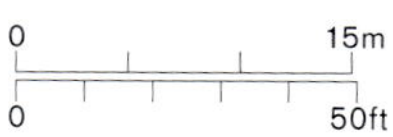

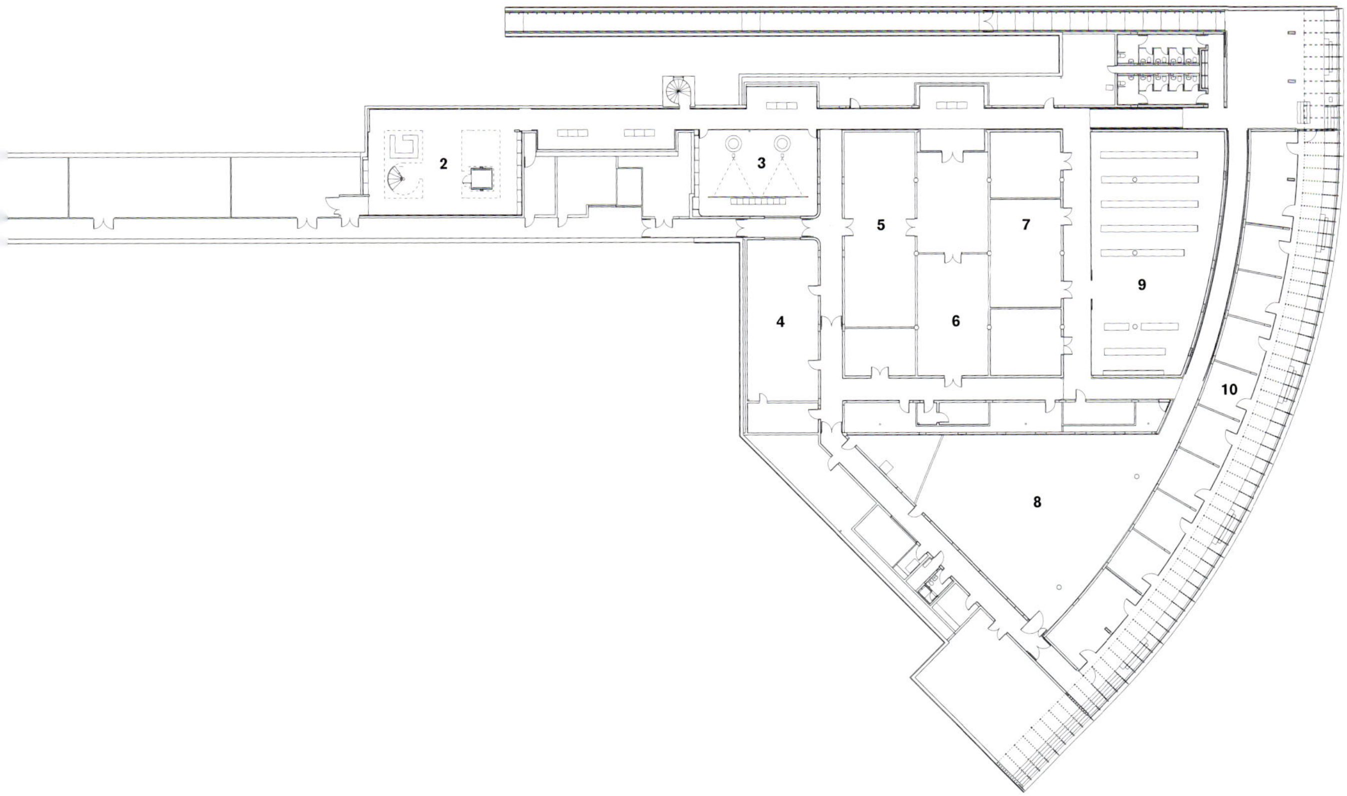
2
3
4
5
6
7
8
9
10

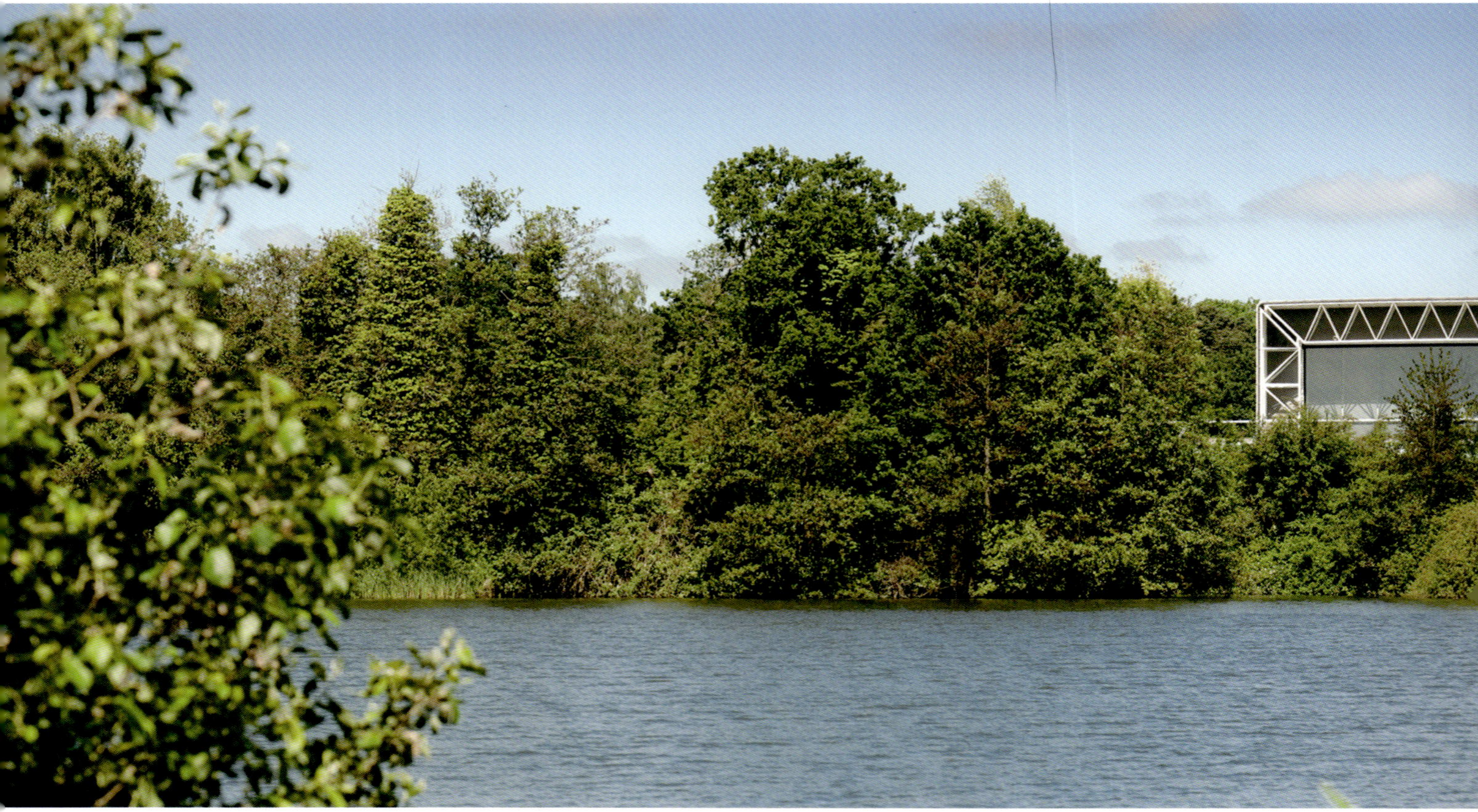

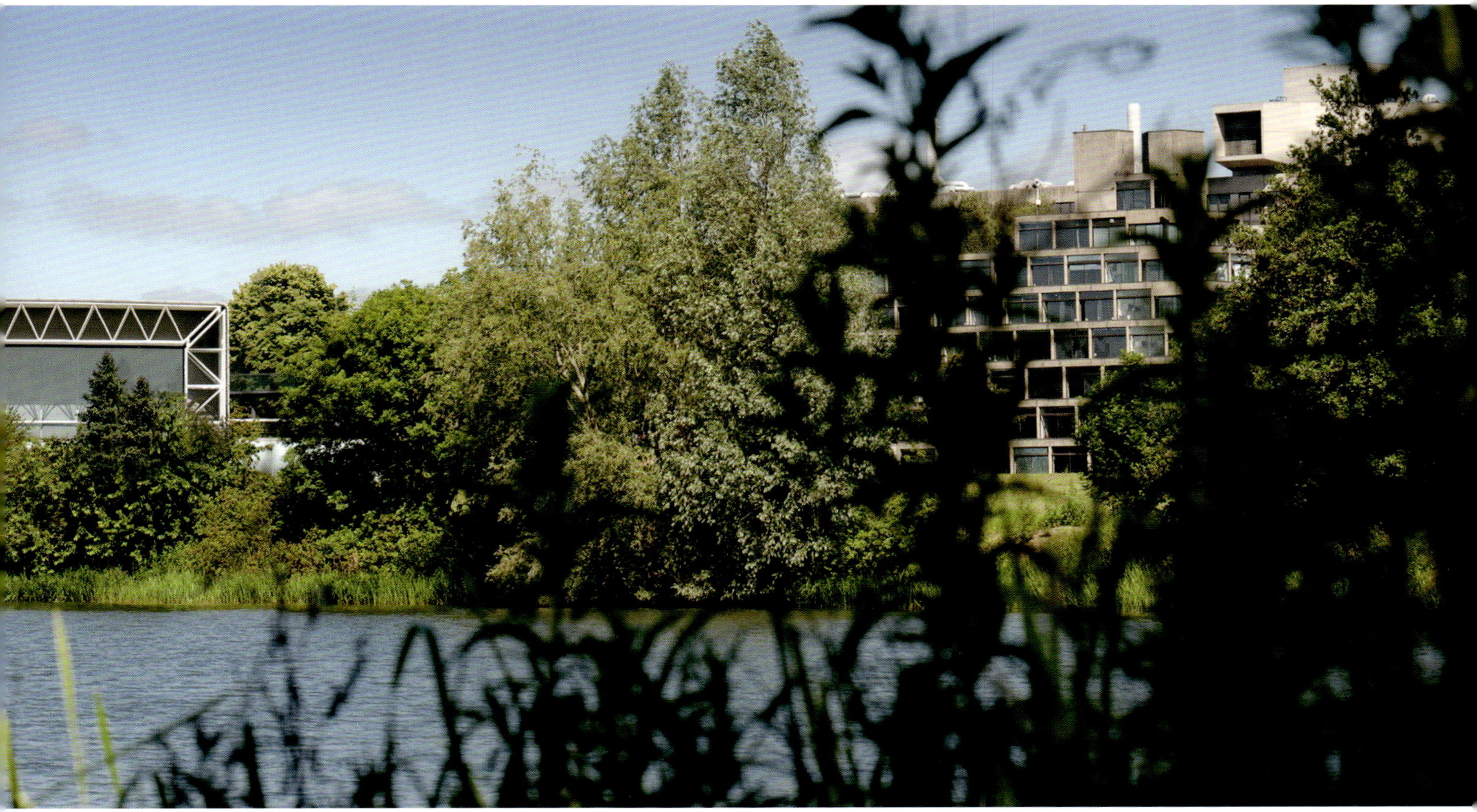

The Sainsbury Centre and Crescent Wing seen from across the broad, a photograph taken in the summer of 2010.

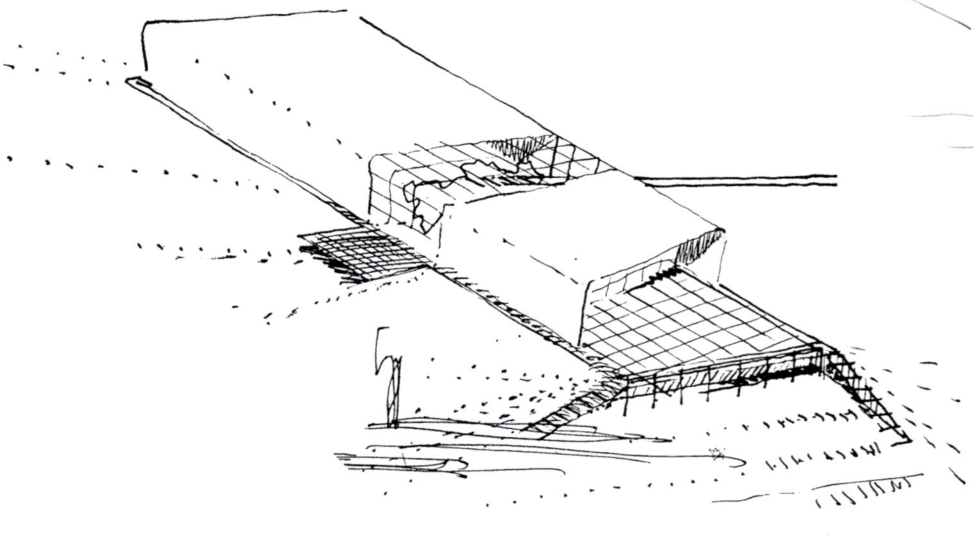

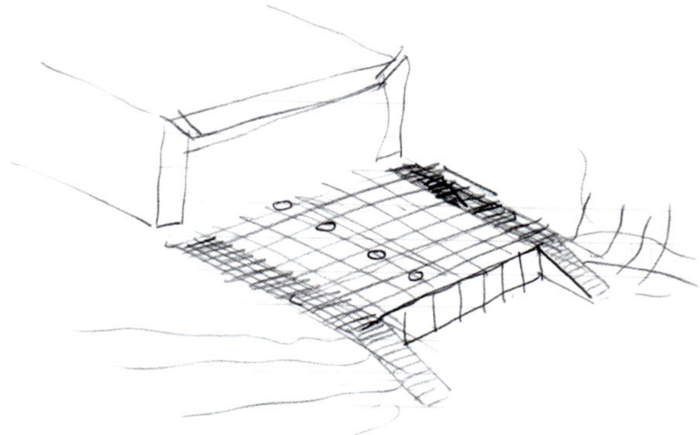

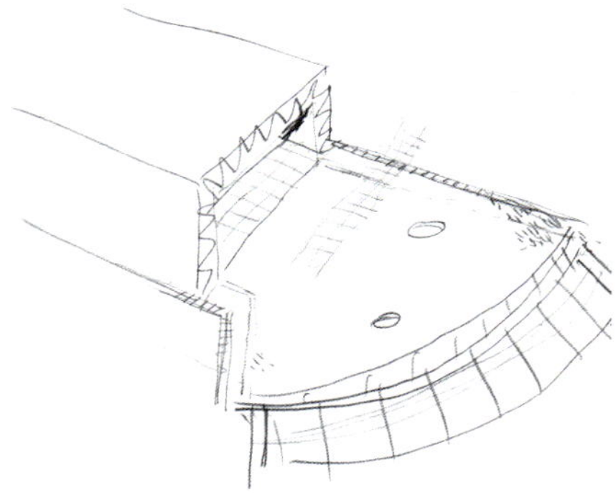

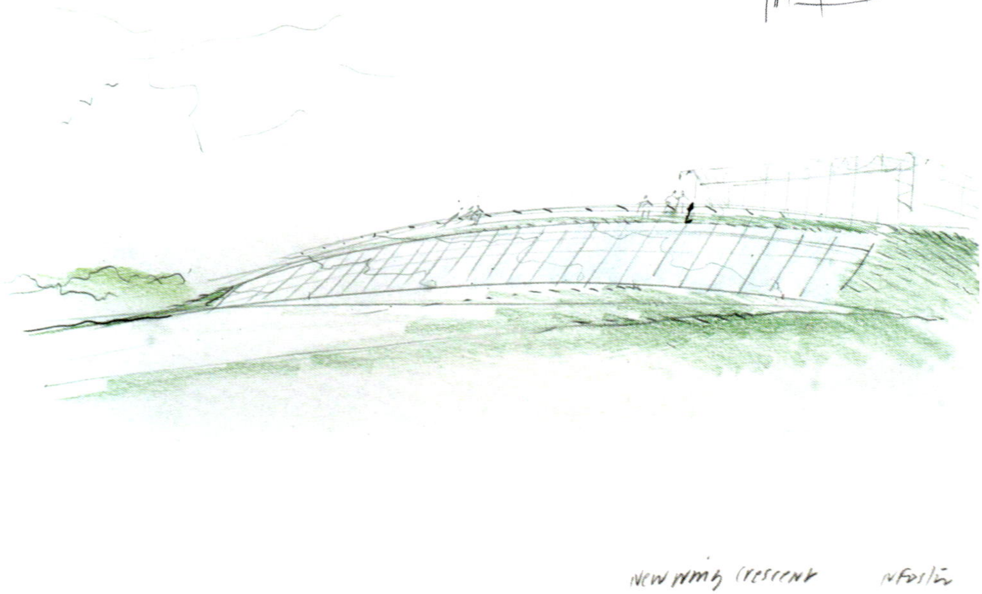

In these sketches, Norman Foster investigates ways of expanding the original building. The premise that the Sainsbury Centre should retain its autonomy, and that the new accommodation provided by the Crescent Wing should be seen as subsidiary, was central to the design process.

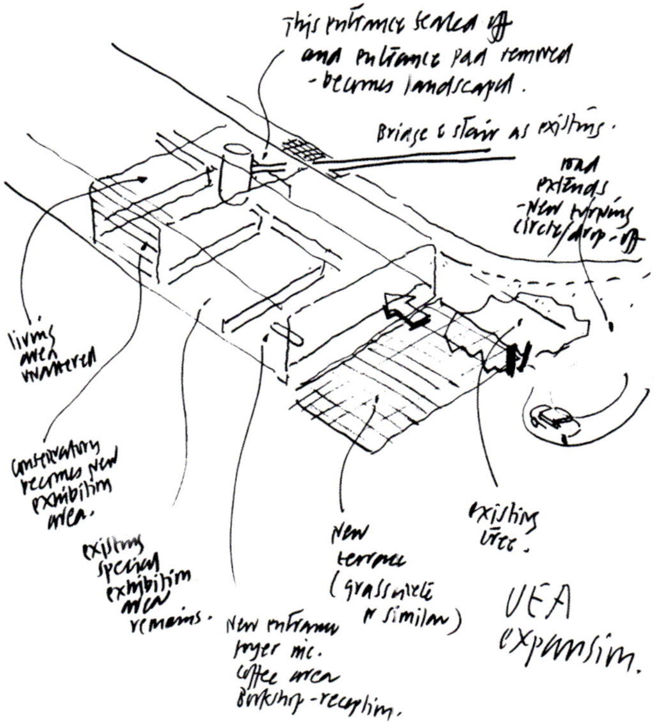
This entrance sealed off
and entrance pad removed
- becomes landscaped.
Bridge & stair as existing.
road
extends
- new turning
circle/drop-off
living
area
unaltered
Conservatory
becomes new
exhibition
area.
existing
special
exhibition
area
remains.
New entrance
foyer inc.
coffee area
bookshop - reception.
New
terrace
(grasscrete
or similar)
existing
tree.
UEA
expansion.

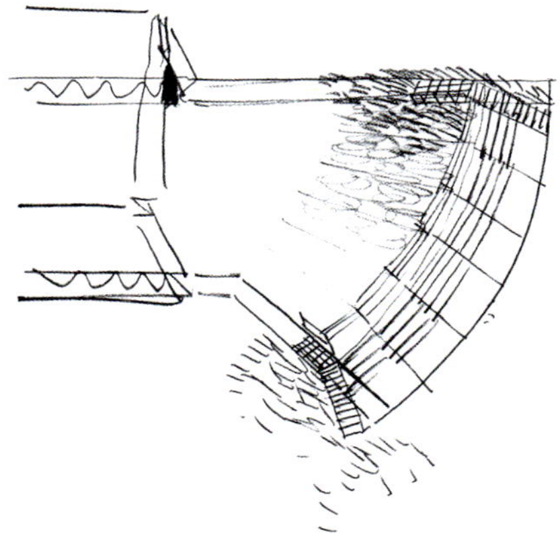

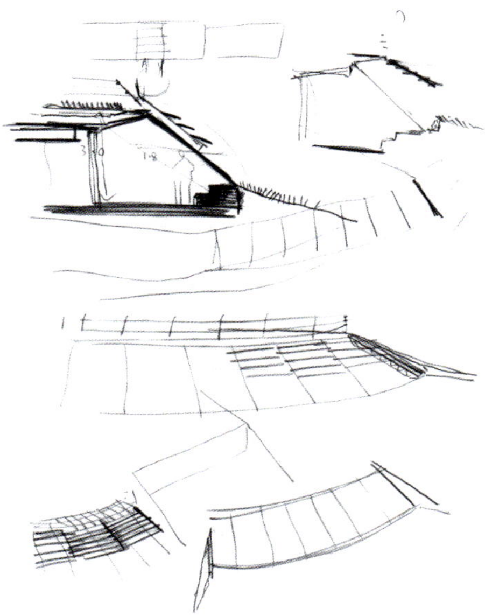

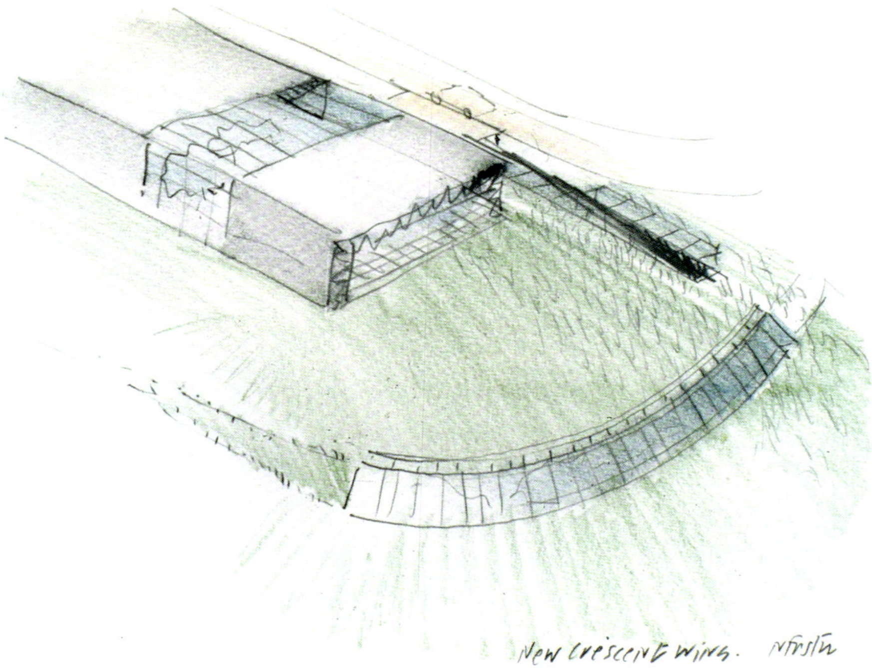
New crescent wing.
NFoster

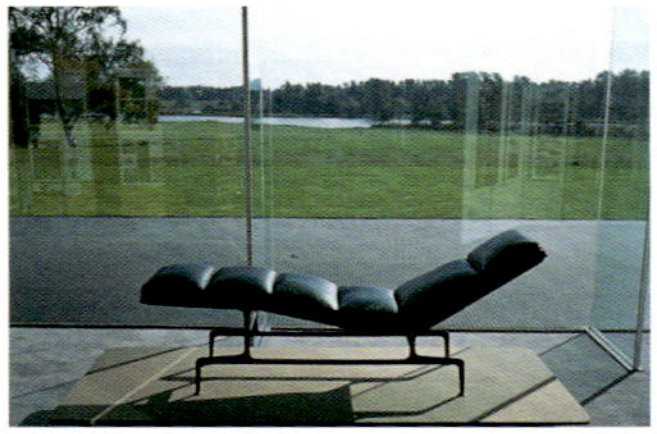

Left: The definitive view from the Sainsbury Centre – looking out through the east portico towards the lake. The challenge in extending the building was to preserve this aspect intact.

– it was possible to dispense with the louvres and to use inclined glazing instead, which is a far more elegant solution. The engineering of this wall was far from straightforward. It was explored in drawings and models, and finally in a full-size mock-up. The glazed elevation had to accommodate a fire escape door, but this was successfully inserted without disrupting the serenity of the great sweep of glass. The final refinement was the provision of bench seating along the inside of the elevation – a perfect place for informal staff meetings.

Perhaps the greatest surprise of the Crescent Wing is the degree to which it is permeated by natural light. The grassed roof is pierced by flush circular roof-lights, which bring daylight into the workshop spaces. Daylight also floods into the depths of the building down the length of the long ramp. In contrast, the lecture room/ gallery space is artificially lit, using a sophisticated lighting system that is adaptable to a wide range of uses and occasions. Lighting elsewhere in the Crescent Wing ranges from recessed uplighters along the entrance ramp to low-voltage spots in the office corridor. (George Sexton as lighting designer provided another element of continuity.)

In assuming a character quite distinct from that of the Sainsbury Centre, the Crescent Wing both acknowledges the classic status of its predecessor and reflects Foster's increasing concern for historic context, which is revealed in projects such as the Sackler Galleries at the Royal Academy in London and the reconstruction of the Reichstag in Berlin. In the case of the Crescent Wing, which opened in May 1991, the fact that the immediate context was an earlier building by Foster himself was immaterial.

Foster's own description of the opposing relationship between the new and the old – the 'cave' and the 'tent' – is telling. The original Sainsbury Centre is notable for its clarity and single-mindedness. The building's founding architectural idea is expressed with a strength of conviction that overrides the conflicting demands of a multiplicity of uses, subordinating all to a remarkable serenity. It sits in the landscape with all the assurance of a Palladian country house. The Crescent Wing, by comparison, is reticent, subtle, complex, linked to its parent building yet with a life of its own. Foster's 'cave' turns out to be a very singular place, where his customary concern for light and space is brought to bear with surprising results. Far from being a retreat from the radicalism of the 1970s, the Crescent Wing holds a special place in the Foster canon as a marker in the practice's increasingly fertile exploration of contextualism and ecology.

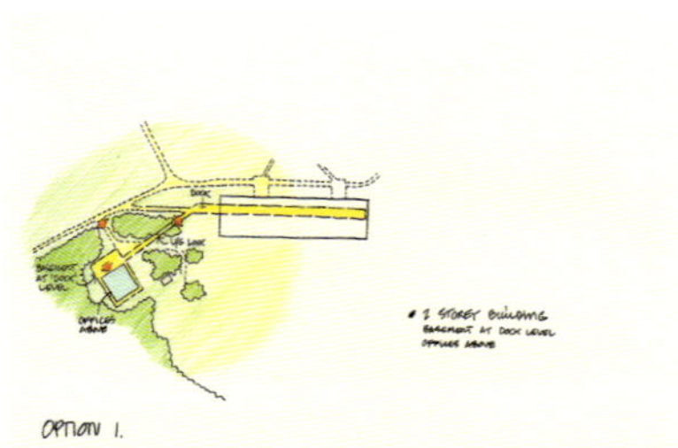

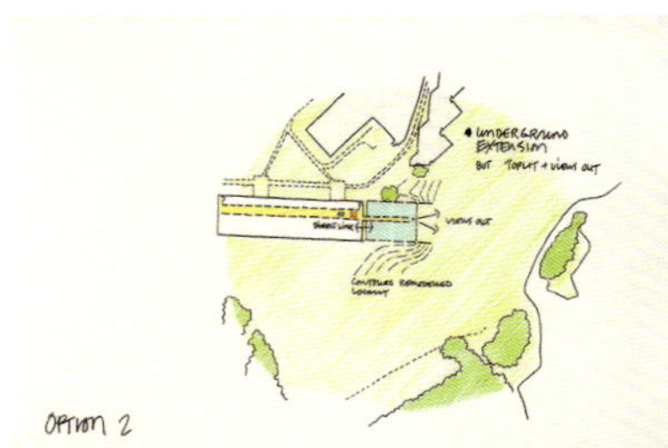

Below: Many options for the extension were explored, including building in the nearby woods, but the idea of an underground development offered greater potential.

Right, far right: Once the idea of a triangular multi-purpose gallery/lecture theatre had been accepted, the planning of the other internal spaces – and their relationship with the day-lit offices that line the crescent – began to fall into place.

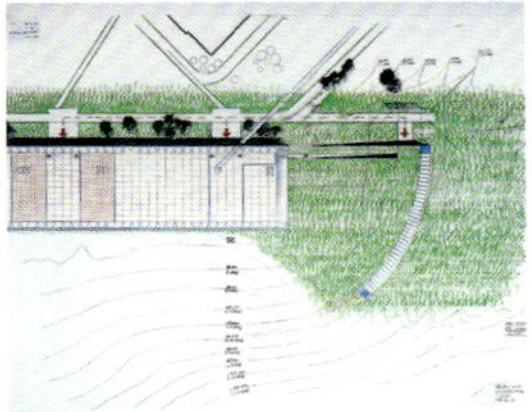

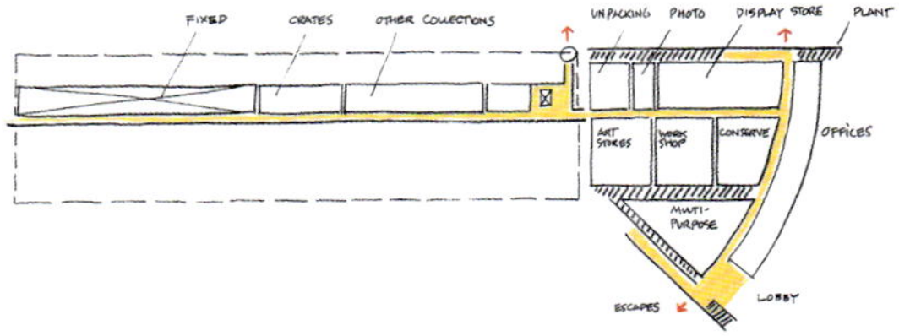

Sir Robert Sainsbury died in 2000. but Lisa Sainsbury has continued her close involvement with the Centre, as has Lord Sainsbury. It was in celebration of Lady Sainsbury's 90th birthday, in 2002, that the most recent phase of work was undertaken.

After more than quarter of a century of use, the weaknesses of the Centre as well as its strengths were apparent. In 1978, for example, there had been no shop, only a very simple café and no dedicated education space for school groups (who visit the building in increasing numbers). All these facilities are now, nearly three decades on, regarded as essential features of almost any museum. The Crescent Wing was a success in its own terms, but was detached from the Centre proper, with a separate entrance that never seemed sufficiently inviting during inclement weather; and while the spinal corridor that ran beneath the building had the potential to form a covered link, it was not suitable for public use. It seemed that the time had come to revitalise, if not to reinvent, the Sainsbury Centre.

In tandem with this exercise, Foster was commissioned to refurbish the building. This involved upgrading all the mechanical and electrical services, and renewing the flooring, lighting, blinds and other fixtures. The extent of the task would necessitate the closure of the building for the first time, from August 2004 until May 2006.

The most dramatic change that resulted was the creation of a new direct public route at undercroft level, with lift and staircase (an extension of the spiral stair from the bridge link), between the main gallery level and the Crescent Wing. The route runs through a new bookshop, link lobby and gallery at basement level, which were formed by excavating beneath the floor of the 'conservatory'. A drawings gallery was created in space formerly occupied by a little-used photographic studio and paint shop; and an education room was formed by extending a former workshop area. As a visitor, it is now possible to trace a route from the Crescent Wing via the gallery 'living area' to the restaurant at the western end of the building, or vice versa, entirely under cover. Achieving all of this, comments Spencer de Grey, who led the design team with Norman Foster, was 'rather more complicated than it might seem. But the result is seamless – you might not notice the join.'

This phase of work on the Sainsbury Centre could be seen as the final realisation of Robert and Lisa's original vision. The turnstiles which originally controlled access have gone. (The Centre had long since stopped charging for admission.) The 'living area' itself has been

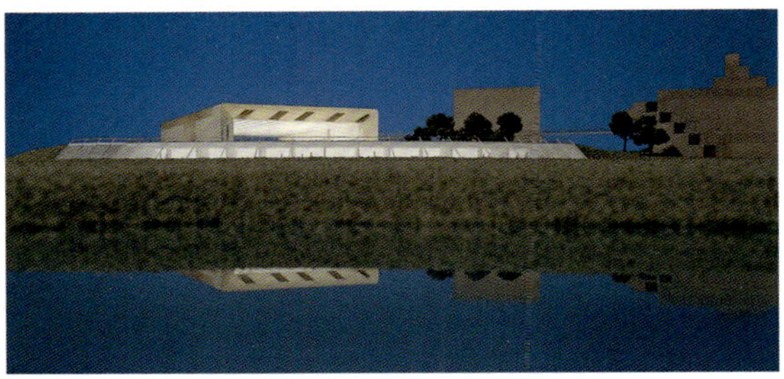

Left: This view of the Crescent Wing model captures something of the drama of the building at night.

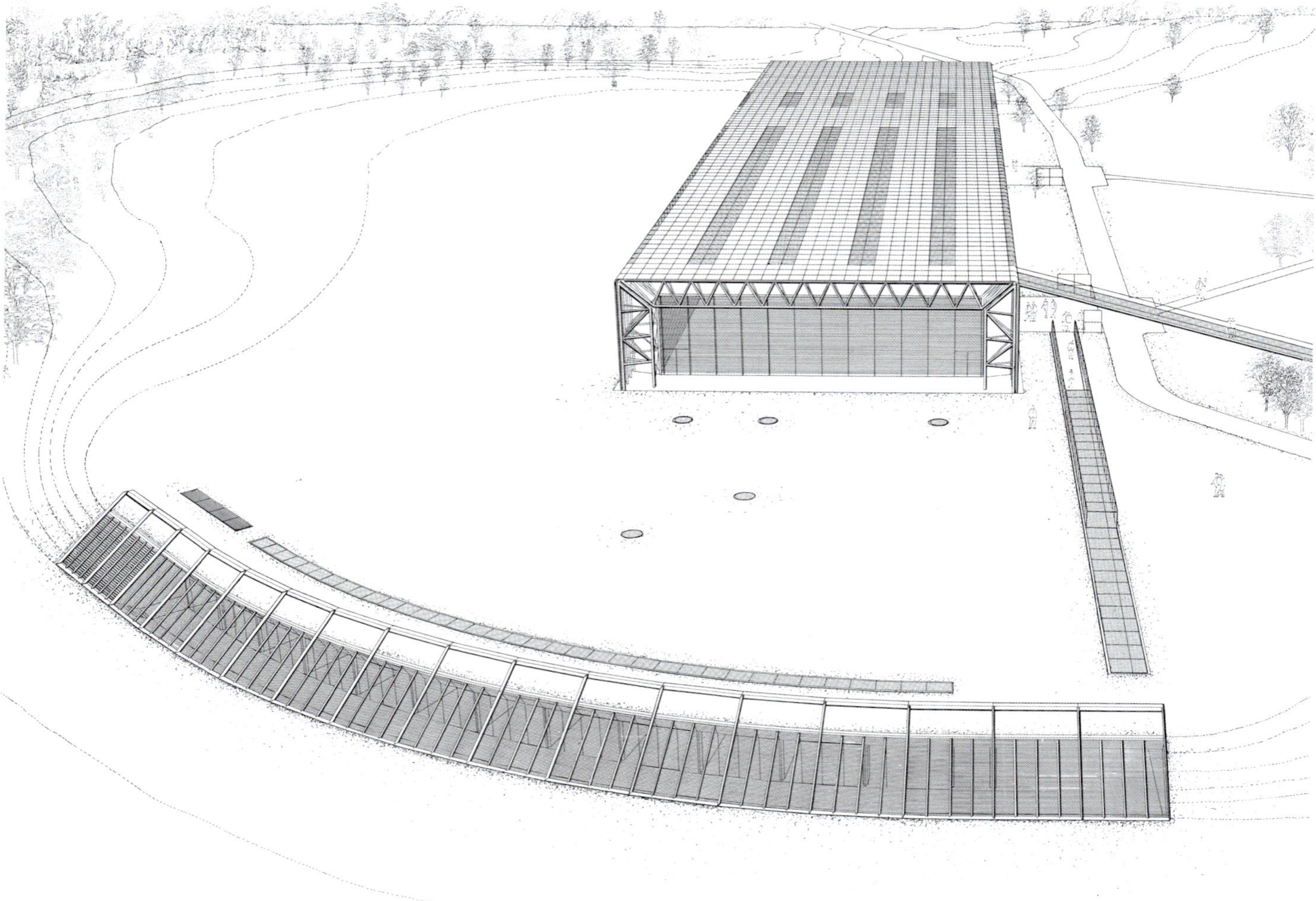

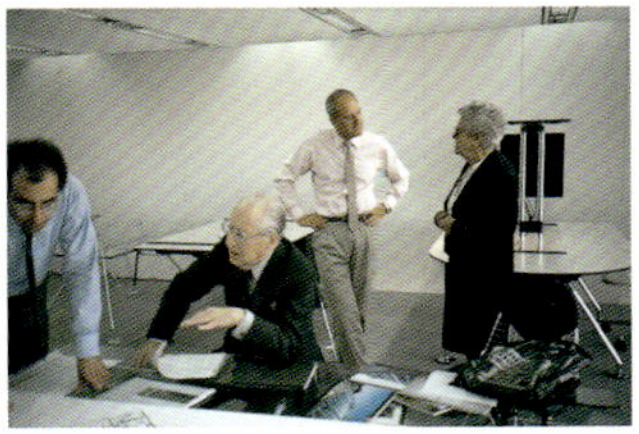

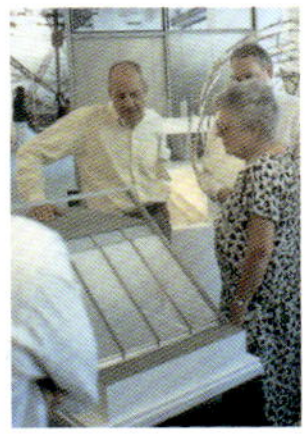

Far left, left: Sir Robert and Lady Sainsbury were closely involved in the design of the Crescent Wing and are seen here in some of the many design reviews.

rearranged, with a clearer visitor route and the introduction of taller display screens at strategic points to provide focal points for vistas across the space.

The two principal entrances to the building have been fitted with canopies and air-lock doors. The reception area has been rearranged and, to the regret of some, the trees which had long been a feature of the conservatory removed. Chris Connell, of Foster + Partners, who ran the project, explains that the modern requirement to limit daylight and humidity levels more strictly – a condition of most loans to temporary exhibitions – meant that the trees could no longer thrive within the building. The small café in the conservatory has been re-equipped, with improved kitchens, and remains a popular lunch spot with both visitors and the university community.

Work on the academic spaces – for what is now the School of World Art Studies and Museology – was completed in 2009. A research area equipped with computer terminals has replaced the former slide library as the hub of the school's accommodation, and gates controlled by swipe cards provide efficient but discreet security.

For Nichola Johnson, the present director of the Sainsbury Centre, the building is 'an aesthetic delight … it's about people having art in their daily lives. The students can just go in and out of the gallery spaces – they can literally get up from their work stations and go and look at something. It's tremendous.' For Johnson, the Centre is not just a continuing resource but also 'an artefact in itself … a total work of art.'

The idea of the Centre as a period piece, a landmark in the history of museology, which it now clearly is, is not something its founders and their architect might have imagined in the heady days of the mid-1970s.

The vision shared by Robert and Lisa Sainsbury and Norman Foster was a radical one, not just in terms of its integration of teaching and research within the context of a public gallery but equally for its insistence that art should be studied and enjoyed in an informal way. Within twenty years this was to become a dominant theme in the development – and redevelopment – of museums across the world. The Sainsbury Centre may have been 'the last word in sleek sheds', the ultimate expression of one phase in the evolution of Foster's architecture and unquestionably one of the few great British buildings of the 1970s. Looking back, however, it was also the first cultural landmark in a growing body of work that would eventually establish Foster as one of the most significant architects of the twentieth century.

Left: An aerial perspective of the Sainsbury Centre and Crescent Wing; the radius of the crescent of glazing matches the site contours as closely as possible.

Right, far right: A cutaway model of the Crescent Wing and a cross section through the perimeter offices and promenade.

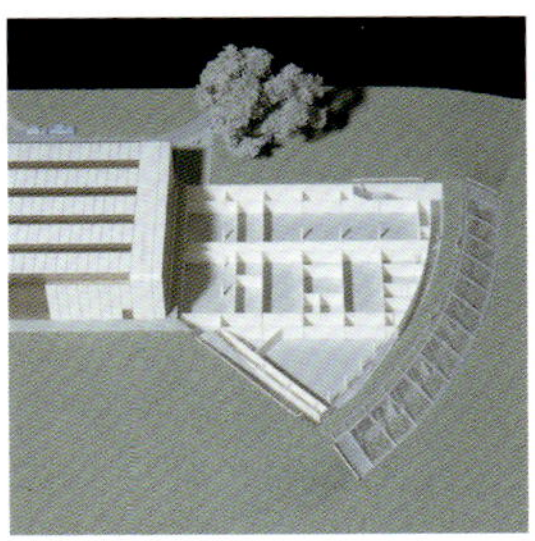

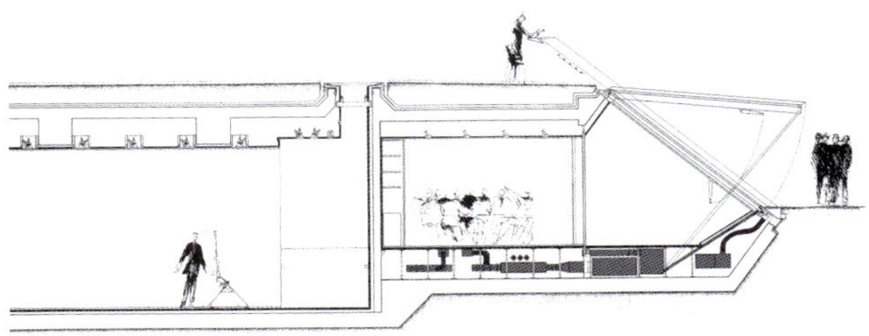

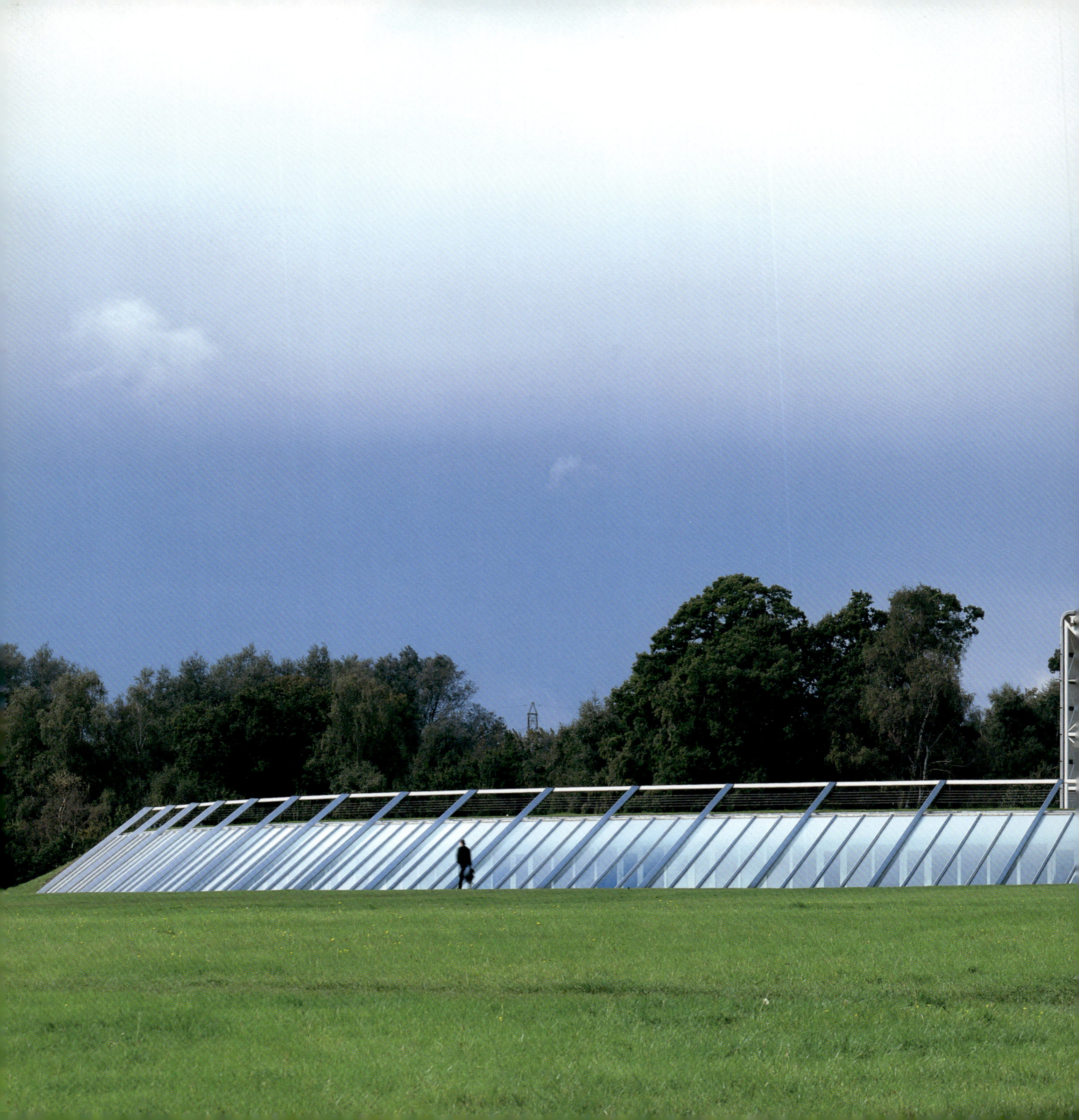

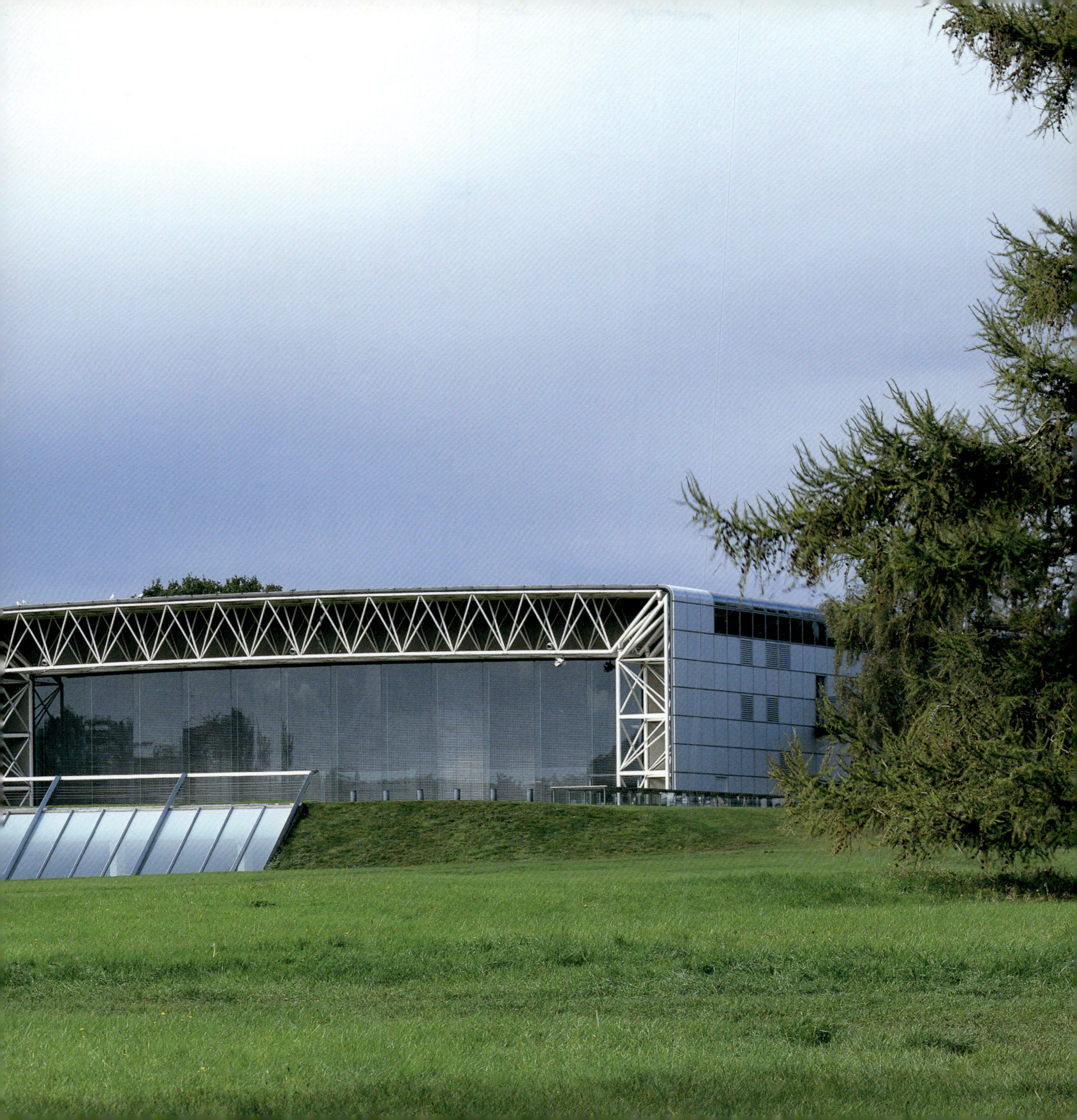

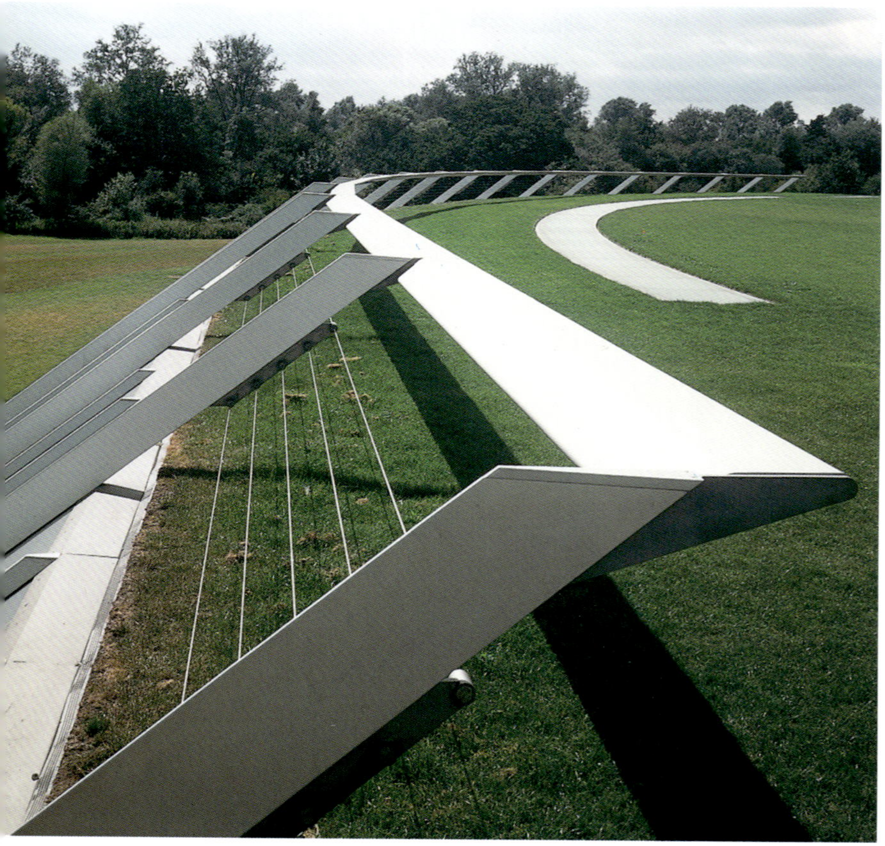

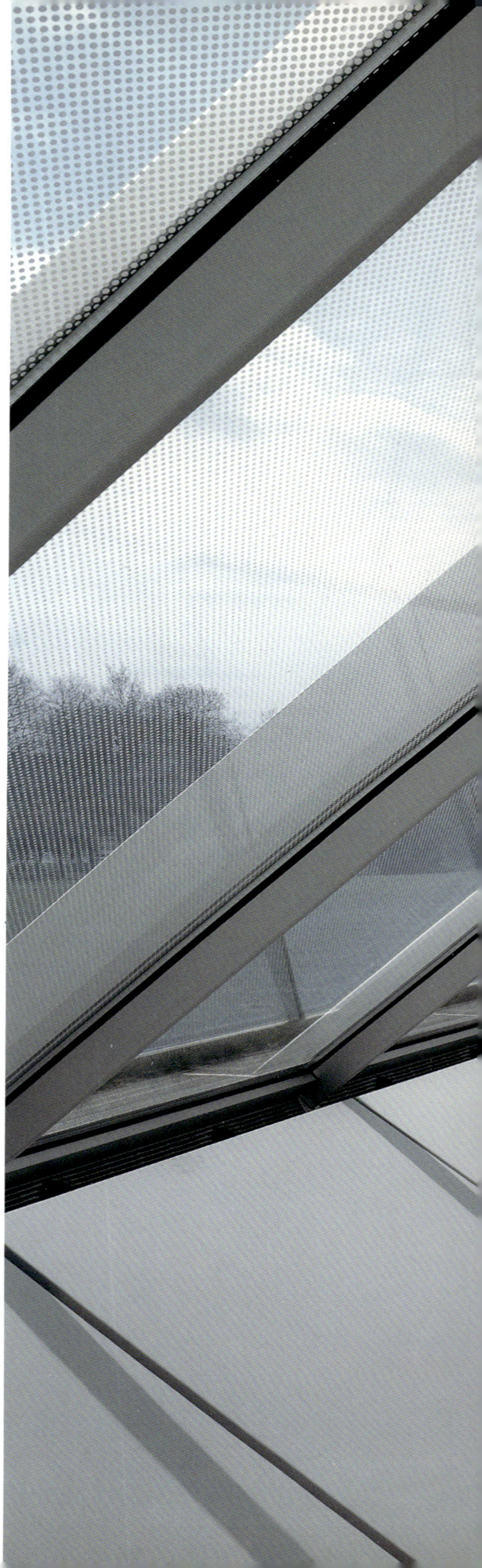

Above: Accentuating the streamlined form of the glass crescent, a handrail was formed by extending the mullions up to meet a wide ledge – perfect for leaning on and enjoying the view.

Right: Looking along the glazed promenade in the Crescent Wing, which provides access to the administrative offices.

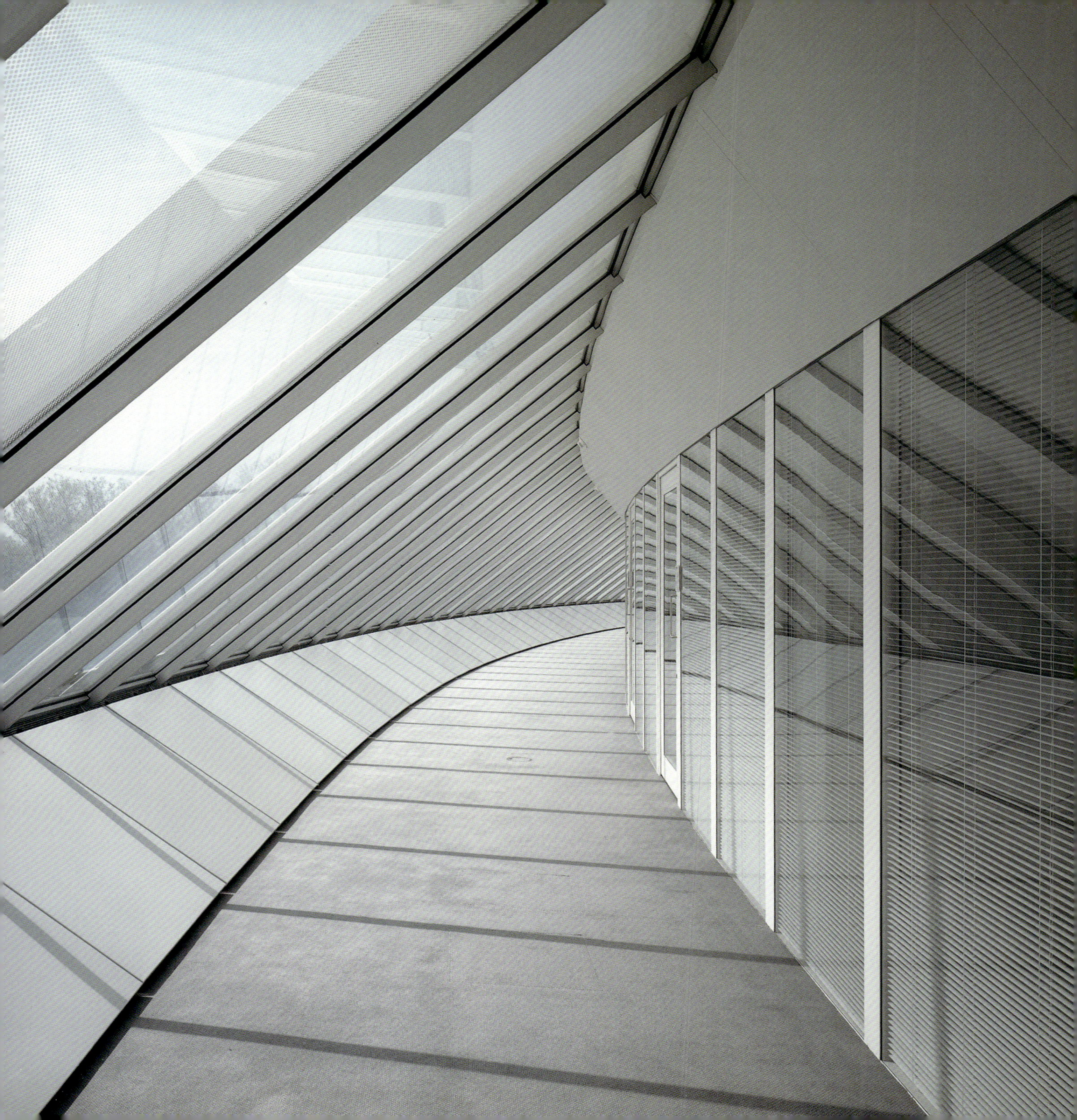

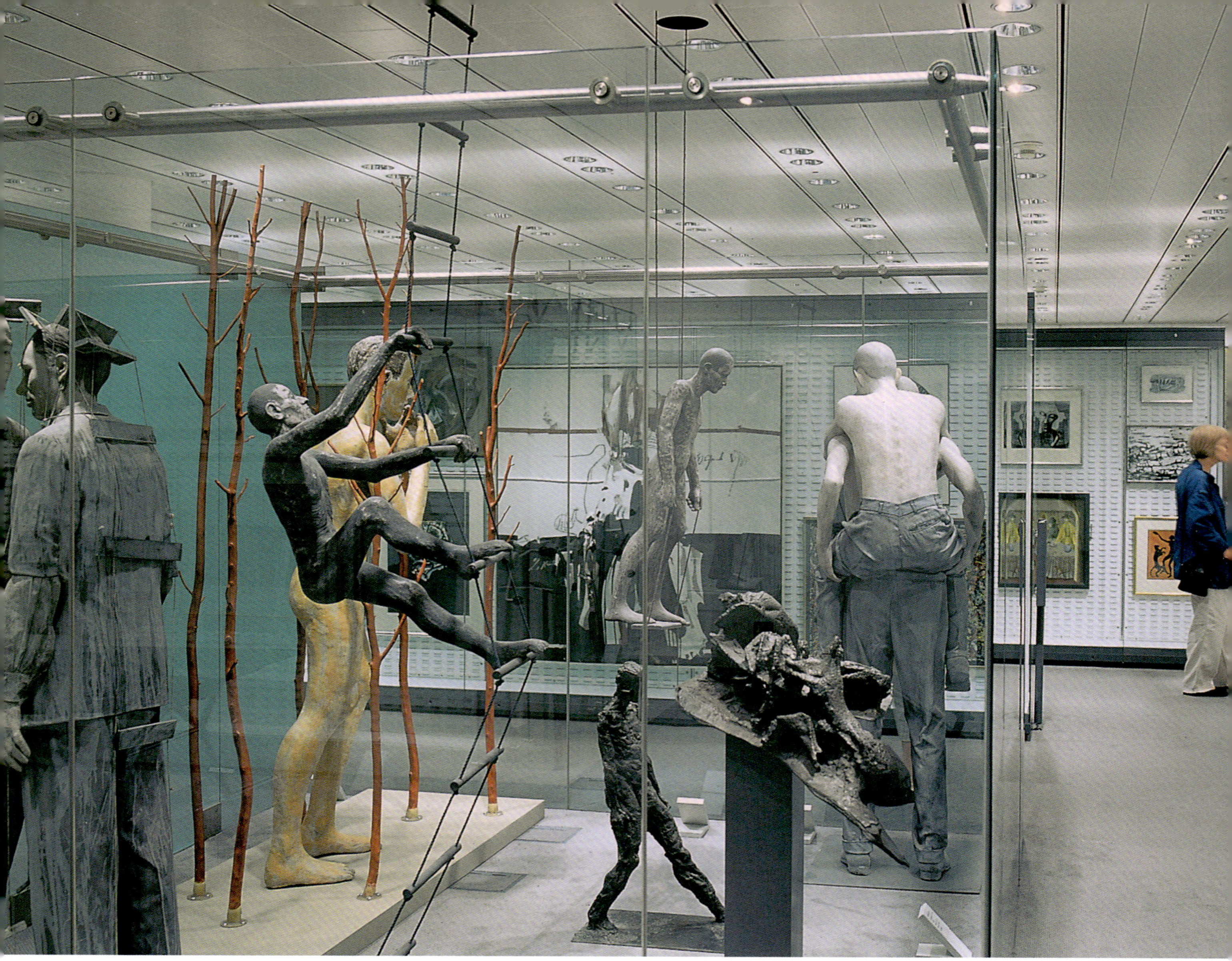

Above and right: The Crescent Wing allowed the expansion of the Sainsbury Centre's reserve study area, workshops and laboratories. Works are housed in optimum environmental conditions in glass cases of various sizes, suitable for two- and three-dimensional pieces, large and small.

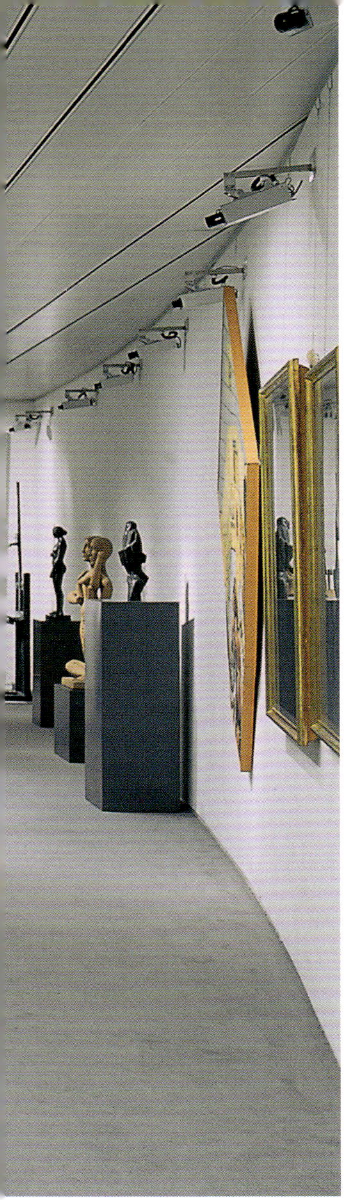

What we have here is a complete suite: a late-1970s building together with a late-1970s display model. It has become very important in the history of collections. Nichola Johnson, Director of the Sainsbury Centre for Visual Arts, 2009

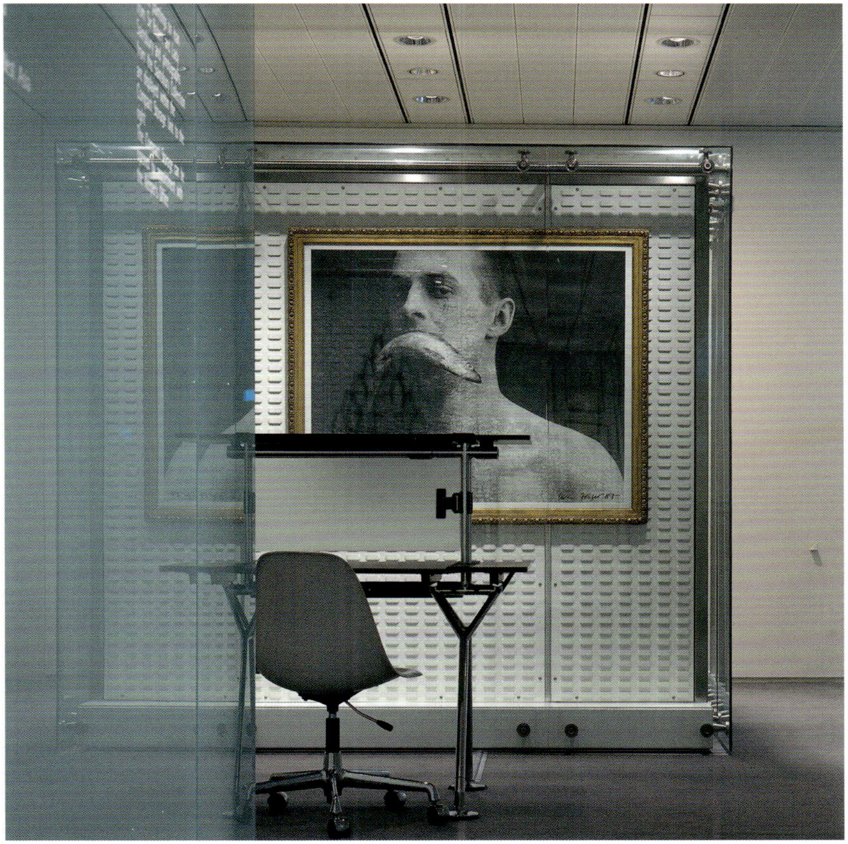

I did not contradict the person who suggested that the building was the greatest work of art in our collection; although I wasn't wildly taken with a lady who looked around the Centre and said, 'It's so beautiful – if only you didn't have these works of art in it'.
Sir Robert Sainsbury, 1983

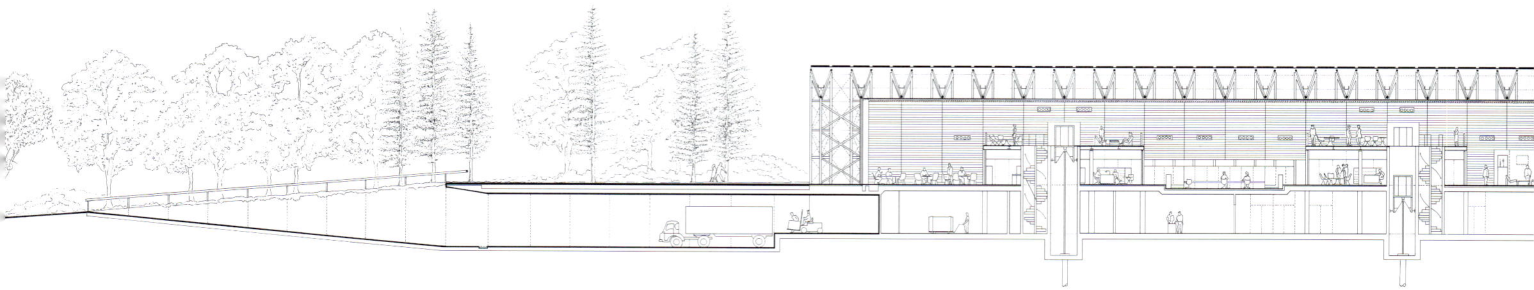

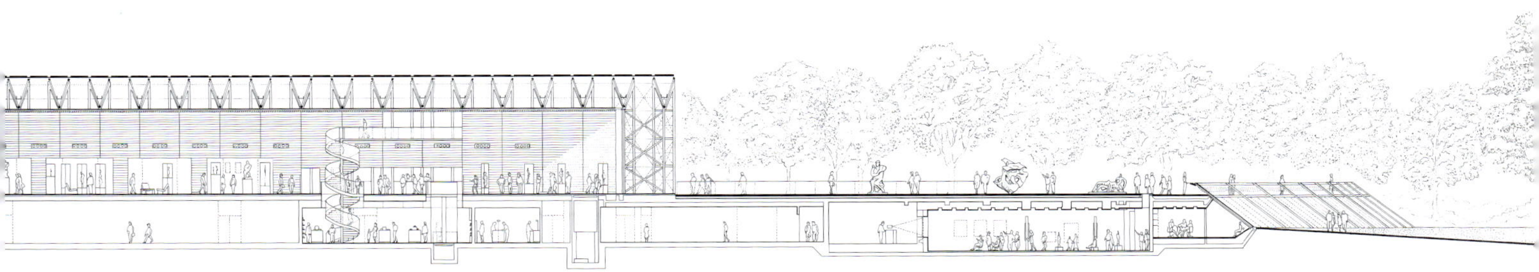

This long section through the Sainsbury Centre and the Crescent Wing demonstrates how the new building forms a logical extension to the existing undercroft. This section shows the building in its most recent form, following the refurbishment of 2006, in which a bookshop and other visitor facilities were introduced at undercroft level.

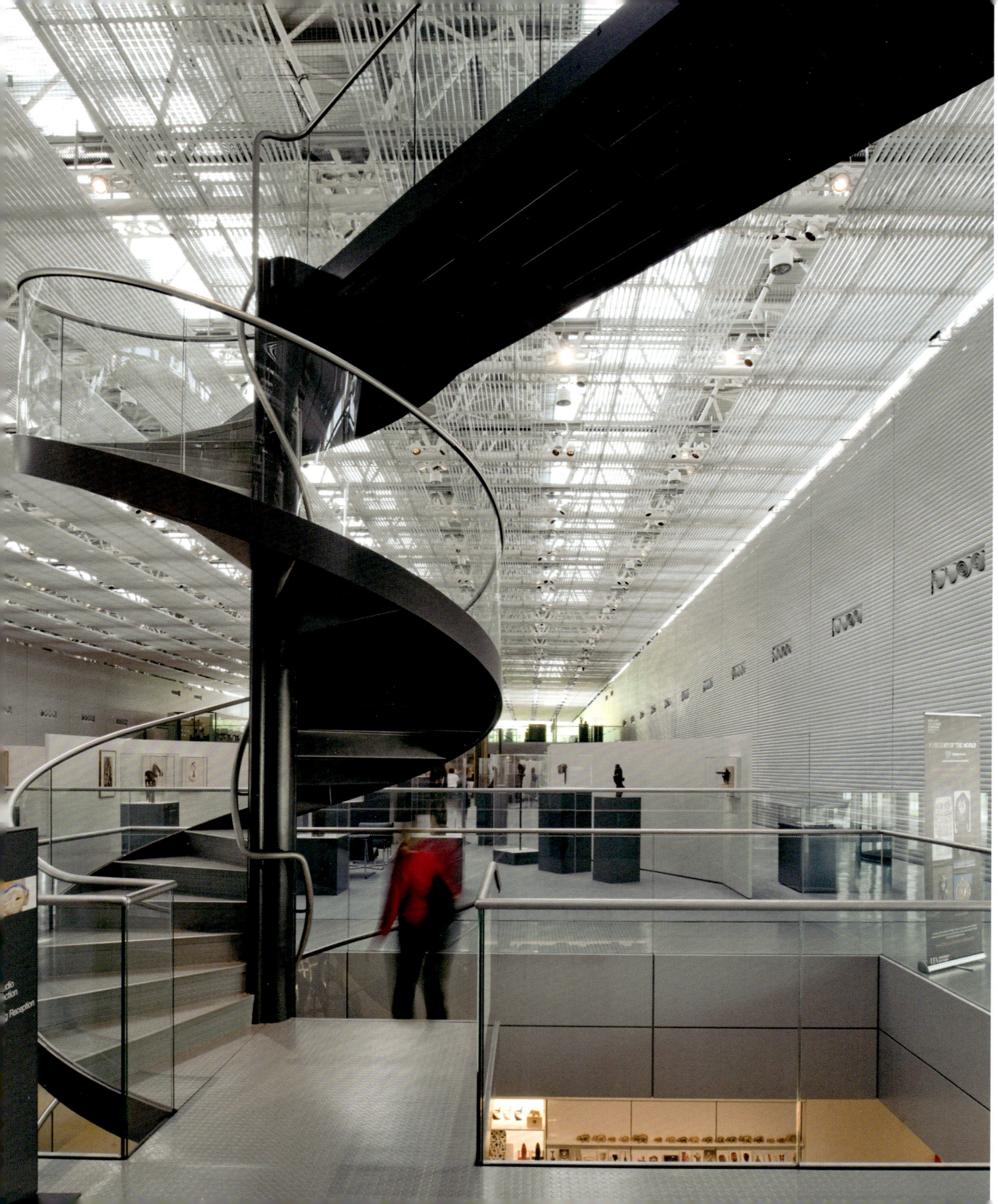

The building is an aesthetic delight. I love walking into it every morning. It is difficult now to understand the impact the building had, particularly in a region like East Anglia where there are no public buildings in the Modernist tradition. Nichola Johnson, Director of the Sainsbury Centre for Visual Arts, 2009

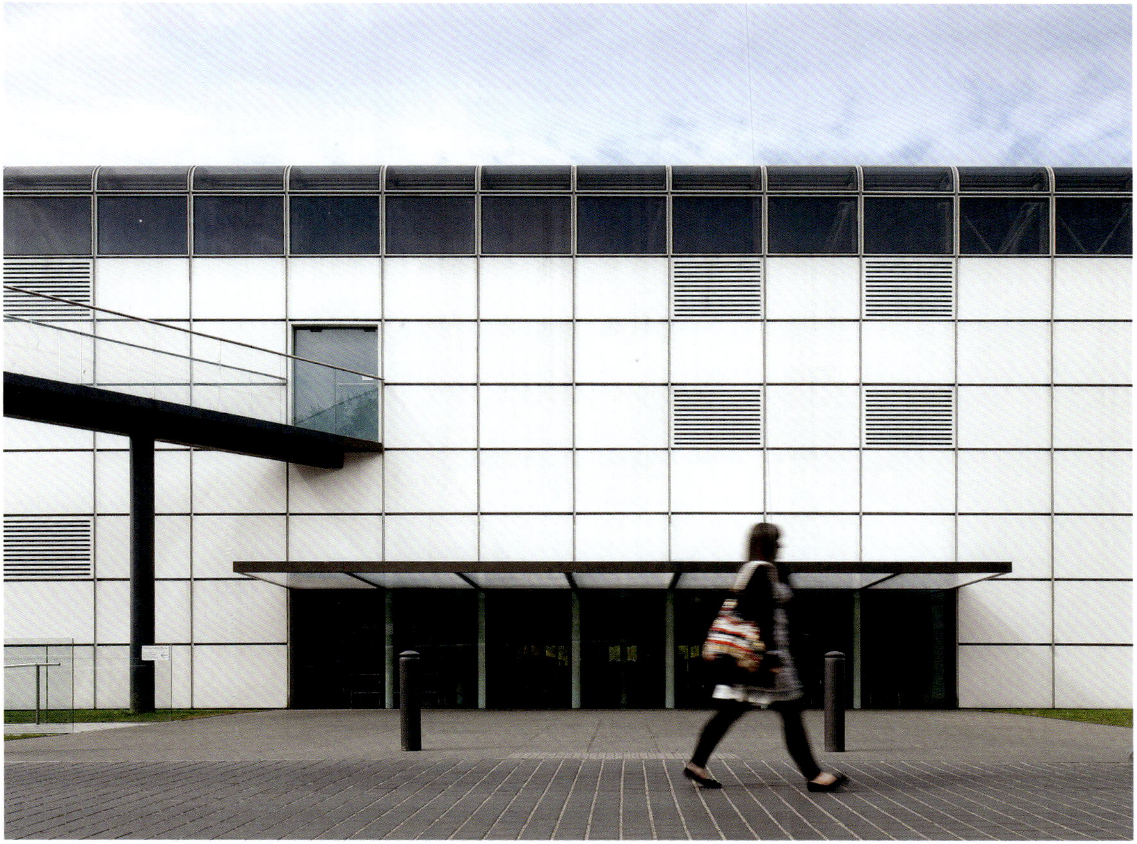

Above: In 2006, glazed canopies were installed above the two entrances – part of a programme of subtle detailed improvements.

Left: As remodelled in 2006, the spiral stair from the bridge link leads down into a bookshop.

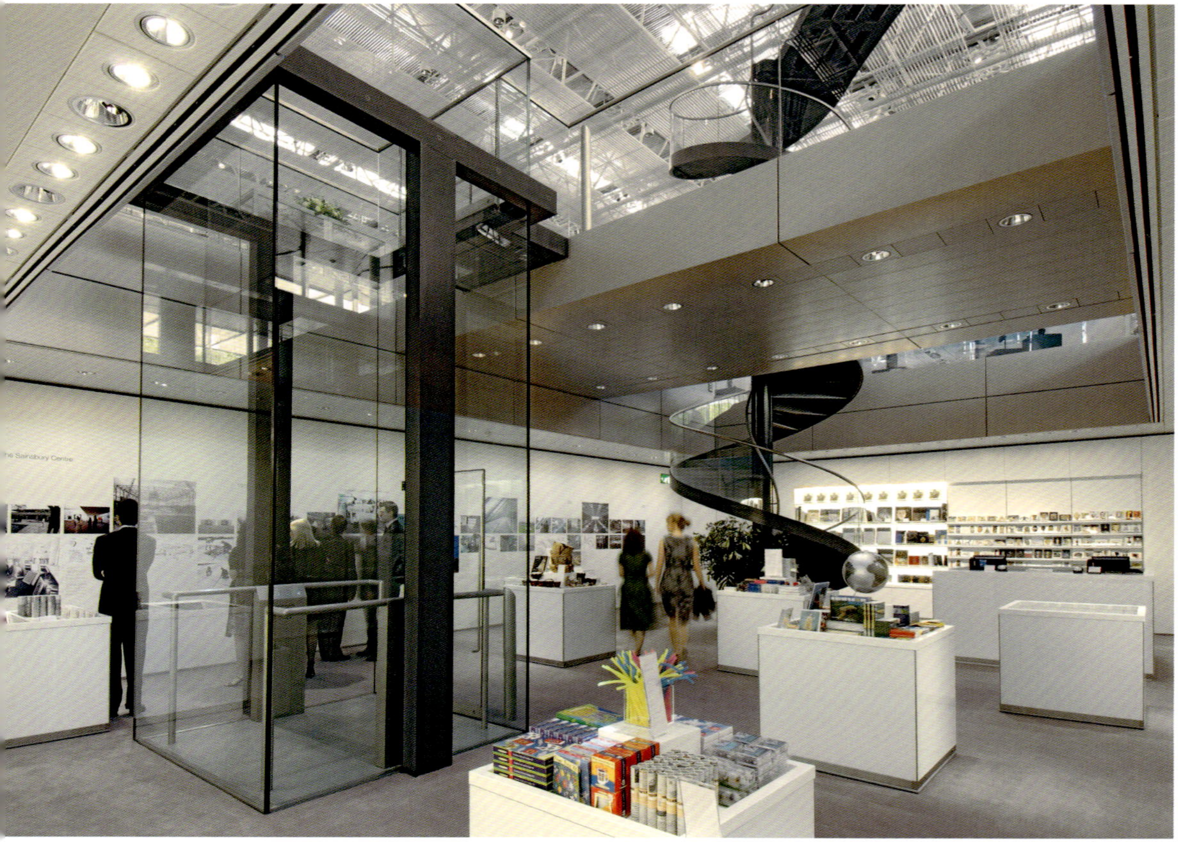

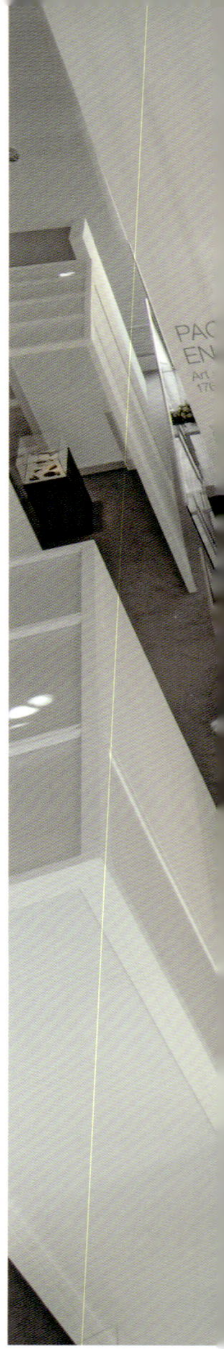

Above: The gallery bookshop at undercroft level.

Above right: Looking down from the bridge link to the reception area, as remodelled in 2006. In place of the conservatory there are new visitor amenities, including a café and bookshop, and a link to the Crescent Wing.

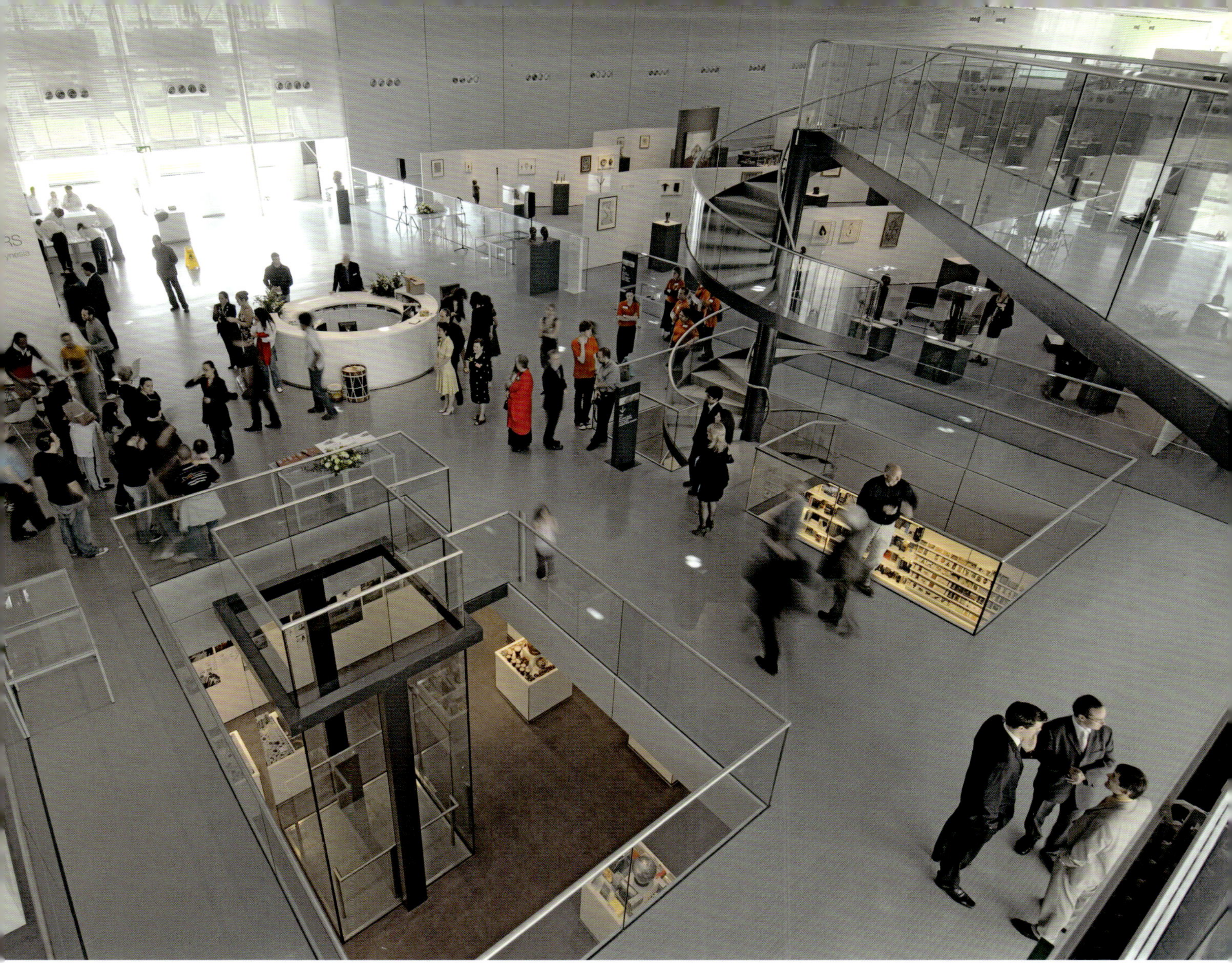

Overleaf: The Sainsbury Centre
and Crescent Wing seen at dusk.

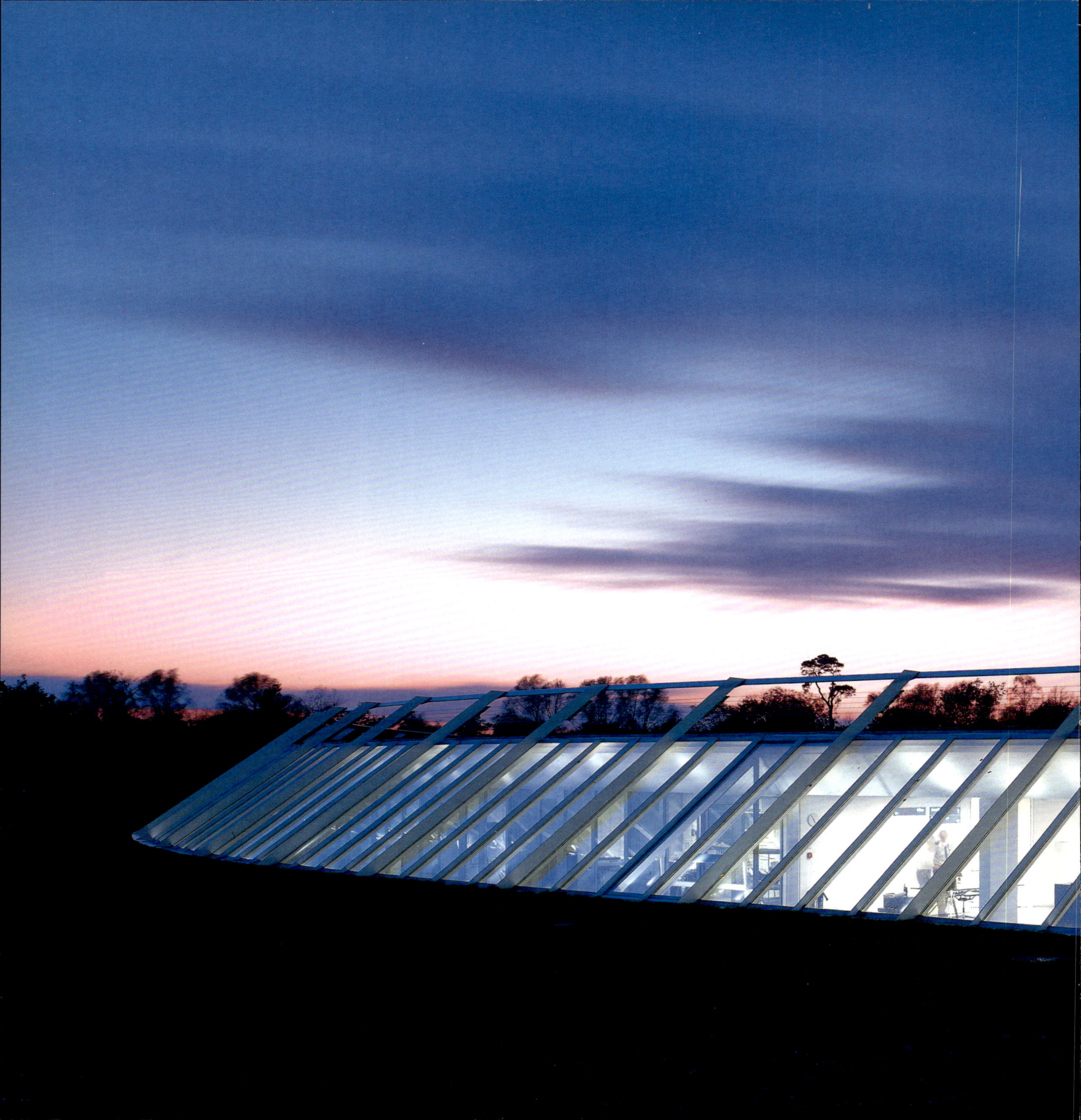

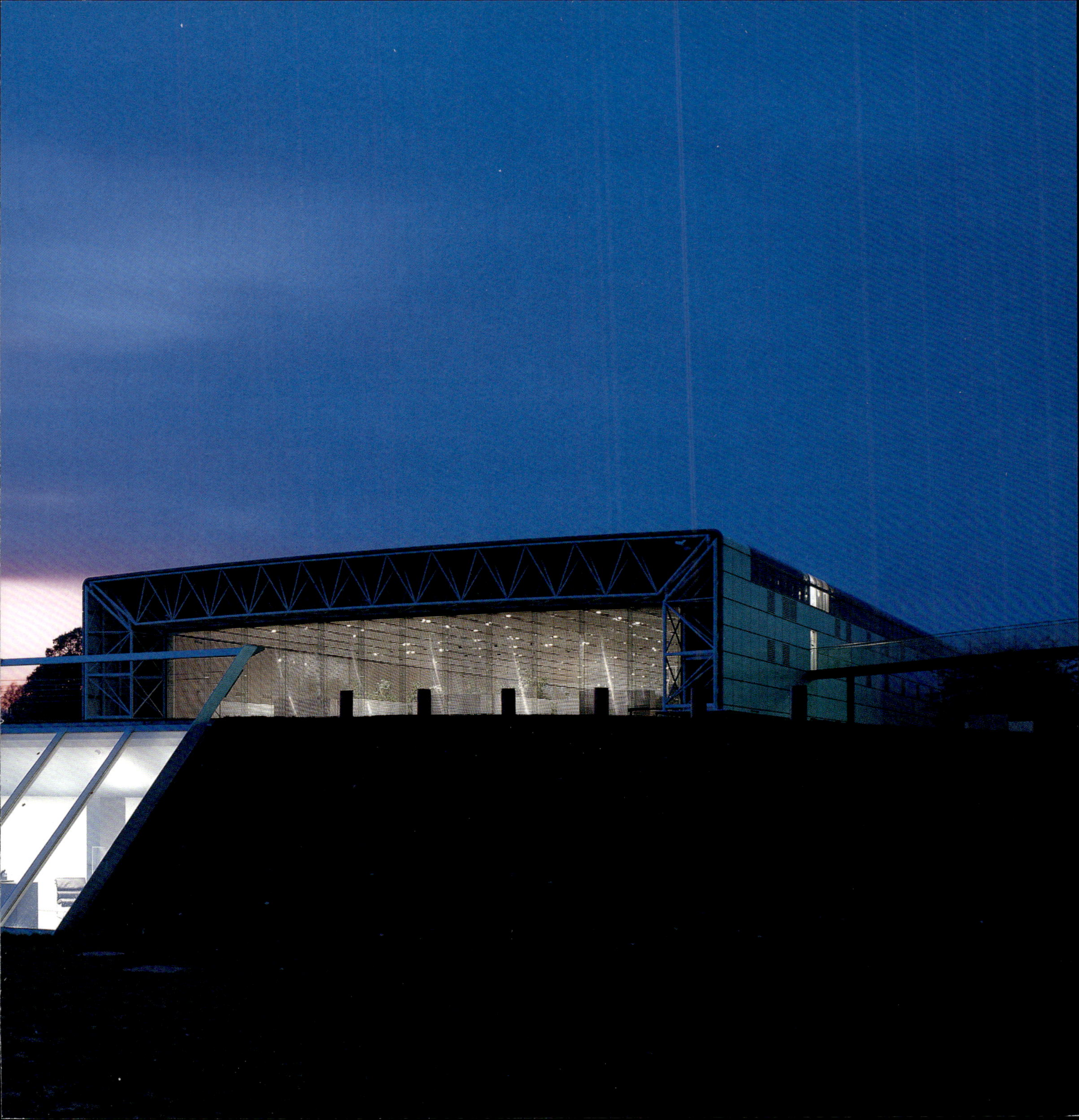

Facts and figures

Sainsbury Centre for Visual Arts
University of East Anglia
Norwich, England
1974 – 1978

Client
The University of East Anglia
Sir Robert and Lady Sainsbury

Project Team
Norman Foster
Wendy Foster

Arthur Branthwaite
Loren Butt
John Calvert
Chubby Chhabra
Spencer de Grey
Jim Elsdon
Howard Filbey
Roy Fleetwood
Diane Haigh
Birkin Haward
Richard Horden
Caroline Lwin
David Nelson
Tomm Nyhuus
Tony Pritchard
Ian Ritchie
Judith Warren
John Yates
Bodo Zapp

Consultants
Structural Engineer: Anthony Hunt Associates
Mechanical and Electrical Engineer: Foster Associates
Quantity Surveyor: Hanscomb Partnership
Lighting: Claude R Engle
Acoustics: Sound Research Laboratories
Landscaping: Lanning Roper
Drainage: John Taylor & Sons
Cladding: Tony Pritchard
Display and Exhibition Lighting: George Sexton III
Graphics: Minale Tattersfield Provinciali

Principal Awards
1978 Structural Steel Finniston Award
1978 RIBA Award
1979 British Tourist Board Award
1979 RS Reynolds Memorial Award
1980 Museum of the Year Award
1980 Ambrose Congreve Award
1980 Sixth International Prize for Architecture (Brussels) Award

Crescent Wing
University of East Anglia
Norwich, England
1988 – 1991

Client
The University of East Anglia
Sir Robert and Lady Sainsbury

Project Team
Norman Foster
Graham Phillips
Chris Connell

Chubby Chhabra
Carsten Grantz
Richard Hawkins
Heiko Lukas

Consultants
Structural Engineer: YRM Anthony Hunt Associates
Electrical and Mechanical Engineers: J Roger Preston & Partners
Quantity Surveyor: Henry Riley & Son
Lighting: George Sexton Associates
Acoustics: Acoustic Design

Principal Awards
1992 Design Review Minerva Award – Commendation
1992 RIBA Regional Architecture Award
1992 Civic Trust Award
1993 Citation Award from the International Association of Lighting Designers

Link gallery and building refurbishment

University of East Anglia
Norwich, England
2002 – 2006

Client
The University of East Anglia

Project team
Norman Foster
Spencer de Grey
Brandon Haw
Chris Connell

Michaela Koster
Andreas Krause
Ben Scott

Consultants
Structural Engineer: Anthony Hunt Associates
Cost Consultant: Davis Langdon
M&E Consultant: Buro Happold
Lighting Consultant: George Sexton Associates
Fire Consultant: Buro Happold
Fire Museum Consultant: George Sexton Associates
Lifts Consultant: Lerch Bates & Associates
Planning Supervisors: PFB Construction Management Services Ltd
Acoustics Consultant: Sandy Brown Associates
Project Manager: Vining Management

Project chronology

1973 26 November: Sir Robert and Lady Sainsbury give virtually all their collection to the University of East Anglia (UEA) and their son David (later Lord Sainsbury) provides a £3m endowment to build the Sainsbury Centre for Visual Arts

1974 1 January: Norman Foster has his first meeting with Sir Robert Sainsbury at 5 Smith Square
28 May: the first design team meeting is held – the design principle is established: 'No excuses – perfection'
October: the architects' brief is received from UEA
October: Norman and Wendy Foster visit the New National Gallery in Berlin, the Aalborg Kunsten Museum of Modern Art and the Louisiana Museum in Denmark, with Sir Robert and Lady Sainsbury

1975 September: the double-skin wall scheme replaces the earlier single-wall scheme

1976 January-March: tender drawings are issued
5 January: preparatory site works are commenced
1 March: Tubeworkers is awarded the contract for the manufacture and erection of all elements of the steelwork
10 May: Tubeworkers begins erecting the steelwork

1978 3 January: construction is completed; the keys are handed over to UEA
4 January: works of art are delivered to the building
4 April: press preview of the Sainsbury Collection
12 April: the Sainsbury Centre for Visual Arts opens to the public

Crescent Wing

1987 12 November: Norman Foster makes an initial presentation to Sir Robert and Lady Sainsbury

1988 March: the brief for the new building is jointly prepared by UEA and Foster Associates
October: a planning application is submitted

1989 February: the management contractor is appointed

1989 May: preparatory works begin on site

1990 9 November: construction is completed; the keys are handed over to UEA

1991 29 May: press preview of the Crescent Wing
30 May: the Crescent Wing opens to the public

Link gallery and building refurbishment

2002 Foster + Partners appointed

2004 2 August: the Sainsbury Centre closes to allow refurbishment and building work

2006 21 May: the Sainsbury Centre reopens to the public

Vital statistics

The Sainsbury Centre and Crescent Wing together have a floor area of 6,000 square metres.

The main permanent gallery, the 'living area', is 1,200 square metres. Additionally, the building provides over 700 square metres of temporary exhibition space – making the Sainsbury Centre one of the largest regional venues for special exhibitions.

Main building
Height: 10.3 metres
Length: 130 metres
Width: 35 metres
Weight: 5,618.6 tonnes

The Robert and Lisa Sainsbury Collection numbers several thousand pieces and features work spanning 5,000 years of human creativity. Modern work by artists such as Henry Moore, John Davies, Alberto Giacometti and Francis Bacon complements art from Africa, the Pacific, the Americas, Asia, Egypt, medieval Europe and the ancient Mediterranean.

The Lisa Sainsbury Collection of Modern Pots includes work from Lucie Rie, Hans Coper and Rupert Spira.

The Sainsbury Centre employs thirty-one permanent members of staff. Additionally, it has sixty volunteers and its activities are supported by a range of specialist freelancers including artist educators, curators, technicians and others.

Two members of staff are dedicated to preserving the collections. Conservation facilities include a laboratory, clean and de-infestation rooms and controlled handling areas.

In addition to its galleries, the Sainsbury Centre building houses two other independent areas of activity: UEA's School of World Art Studies and Museology, including the Sainsbury Research Unit and Museology units; and the gallery café and restaurant.

The Sainsbury Centre galleries attract 40,000 visits a year to exhibitions and events, 10,000 of which are made by young people in school groups. The galleries, café, restaurant and School of World Art Studies are used by over 150,000 people every year.

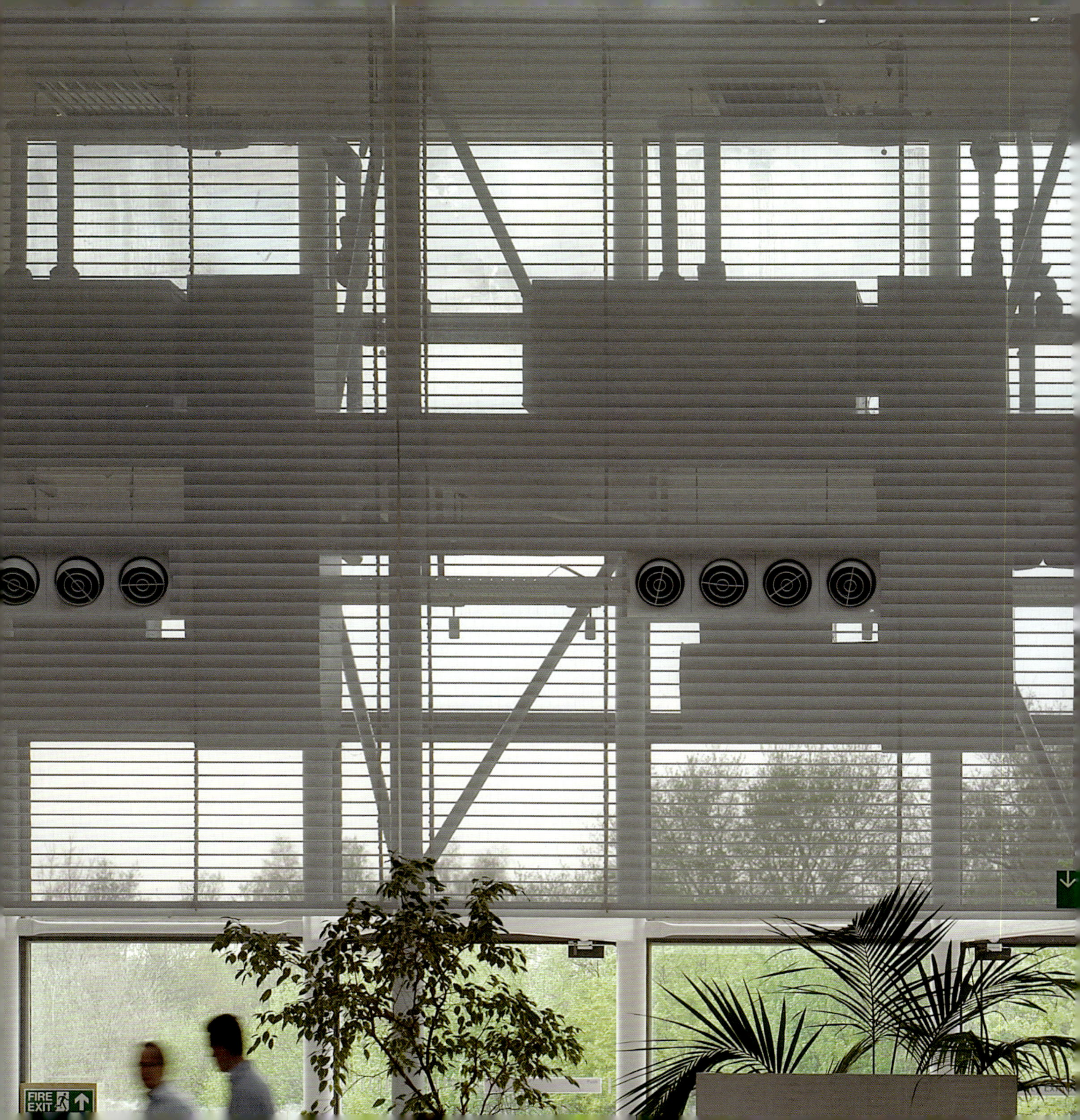
FIRE
EXIT

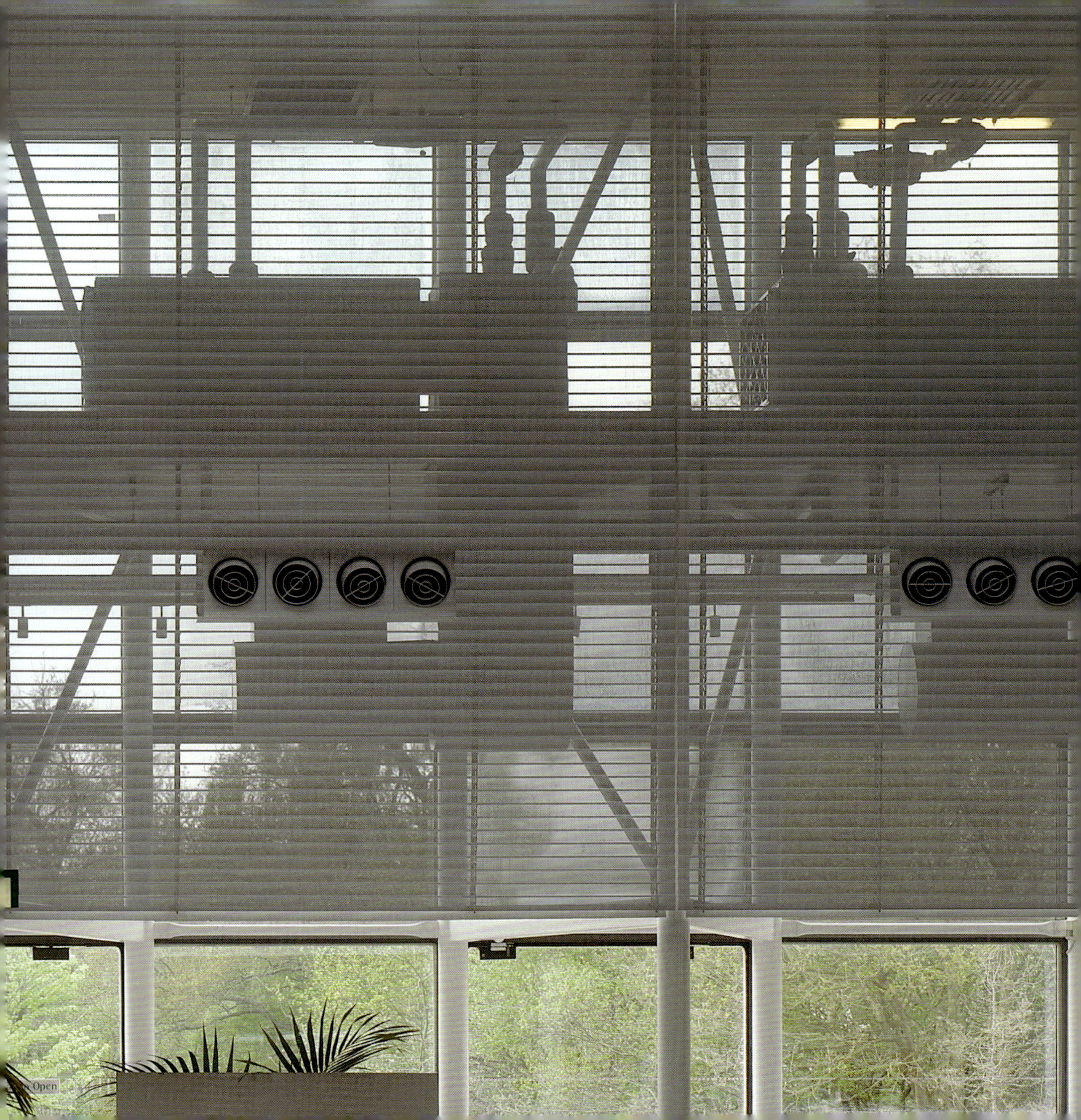
Open

Credits

Editor: David Jenkins
Design: Thomas Manss & Company; Thomas Manss, Enrica Corzani, Keira Yang
Picture Research: Kathryn Tollervey, Gayle Mault
Proofreading: Julia Dawson, Rebecca Roke
Production Supervision: Martin Lee
Reproduction: DawkinsColour
Printed and bound in Italy by Grafiche SiZ S.p.A.

The FSC-certified paper gardamatt has been supplied by Cartiere del Garda S.p.A., Italy

FSC
www.fsc.org
MISTO
Carta da fonti gestite in maniera responsabile
FSC® C005613

Picture credits

Photographs
Archive of the Luftschiffbau Zeppelin GmbH Friedrichshafen: 26 (1)
Estate of Francis Bacon, Courtesy of DACS: 14 (1, 2)
Richard Bryant/Arcaid: 51
Peter Cook/VIEW: 81
Richard Davies: 25 (3), 38 (1), 73, 75 (3), 79,
John Donat: 16, 17 (2, 3), 22, 23, 34 (2),72
Norman Foster: 18, 19, 49
Foster + Partners: 29 (1), 49 (2), 75 (1, 2)
Dennis Gilbert/VIEW: 78, 88-89
Alan Howard: 28, 29 (2)
Ken Kirkwood: 6-7, 21, 25 (1), 26 (2), 30-31, 34 (1), 35, 36, 37(1), 40, 41, 42, 48, 49 (1), 50, 51, 52, 53
LAT Photographic: 38 (2)
Robert and Lisa Sainsbury Collection, University of East Anglia/James Austin: 17 (1)
Camera Press, Lord Snowdon: 15 (3)
The Flight Collection: 24
Nigel Young/Foster + Partners: 25 (2), 43, 44-45, 54, 55, 56, 57, 60-61, 64-65, 68-69, 76-77, 80, 84, 85, 86, 87, 94-95

Drawings and Sketches
Birds Portchmouth Russum: 32-33, 39 (2, 5), 82-83
Foster + Partners: 21, 22, 24, 27 (1), 37 (2), 47 (2), 72, 73 (2), 74
Norman Foster: 4, 5, 20, 25 (5), 27 (2), 49, 50, 70, 71, 73 (1), 75
Gregory Gibbon: 12-13, 39,
Birkin Haward: 46, 47 (1)
John Hewitt: 39 (1), 58-59, 62-63, 66-67
Anthony Hunt: 23

Editor's note

In editing this book I am particularly grateful to Norman Foster and Kenneth Powell for their invaluable contributions; to Nichola Johnson and the staff of the Sainsbury Centre for Visual Arts; and to Loren Butt, Birkin Haward and Tony Hunt. I would also like to thank Thomas Manss, Enrica Corzani and Keira Yang for bringing the book to life graphically; Kathryn Tollervey and Gayle Mault, who mined the office archive; Julia Dawson and Rebecca Roke for proofreading the text; Martin Lee for coordinating production; and the numerous people in the Foster studio – past and present – who helped piece together the background to the project.

David Jenkins
London, August 2010